Past-into-Present Series

BUILDINGS

Alan James

B T BATSFORD LTD, London & Sydney

First published 1975
© Alan James 1975

ISBN 0 7134 3049 4

Printed by The Anchor Press, Tiptree, Essex
for the Publishers B T Batsford Ltd
4 Fitzhardinge Street London W1H OAH
23 Cross Street Brookvale NSW 2100 Australia

For Patience and Cyril and Scalby Beck

Acknowledgment

The Author would like to thank E C Watkinson, Dip Arch., RIBA, for his kindness in providing technical advice.

The Author and Publishers would also like to thank the following for their kind permission to reproduce copyright illustrations: Cyril Butler for figs 13, 16, 36, 38, 50, 53, 54, 55, 56, 65; the Post Office for fig 61; Architects' Journal for fig 60; the Radio Times Hulton Picture Library for figs 1, 4, 5, 6, 19, 20, 22, 25, 27, 29, 30, 33, 34, 35, 37, 39, 40, 41, 42, 43, 46, 47, 48, 49, 51; J Peterson for fig 2; Edwin Smith for fig 7; Department of the Environment for fig 8; A F Kersting for figs 9, 14, 21, 24, 26, 31, 32; Herbert Felton for fig 17; J Allen Cash for fig 23; Leonard and Marjorie Gayton for fig 28; Middlesbrough Public Library for fig 44; Salford Public Library for fig 45; Keystone Press Agency for figs 52, 57, 58, 59, 62, 64; *Evening Chronicle,* Newcastle, for fig 63. The other pictures appearing in this book are the property of the Publishers.

Contents

List of Illustrations

Introduction

Domestic architecture began when the first simple hut was built to provide shelter from wild beasts and the elements — rain, wind, frost, snow, and the burning sun. Thousands of years have since passed, during which houses have improved in comfort and convenience, as well as in hygienic conditions and architectural attractiveness.

Improved building materials and new methods of construction — reinforced concrete and steel-framed buildings, for instance — have resulted in recent years in the emergence of high-rise blocks and other ambitious projects. The busy conditions of modern living necessitate the construction of many types of buildings, each erected for a specific purpose — houses, flats, offices, factories, hotels, cinemas, supermarkets, theatres, department stores, churches, pubs and multi-storey car parks, to name but a few.

There are social, political, economic and climatic reasons for the variety in buildings through the ages. Architecture is, in fact, a reflection of what is happening in history. Almost all buildings are erected to solve the problems of shelter or to protect someone or something from the climate or from other people. To this end the architect has two main tasks: to plan the interior and design the exterior.

This book traces the history of buildings from early times up to the twentieth century, and looks at the architects who conceived them and the builders and masons who constructed them. It is a long road from Stonehenge to the Post Office Tower. At some times buildings seem to have been designed primarily for looking at, and at others for living or working in. Modern architecture and building techniques attempt to combine both aspects, providing first and foremost a 'functional plan', but one which is also attractive to look at. Buildings, after all, can fall into three groups — those serving a useful purpose, those that are decorative and those that combine both of these attributes.

1. Ancient Buildings

Stone Age Tribe, 1971

In the thick mountain forests of the Philippines a tribe of 24 people was discovered in 1971. The tribe of Tasadays live a Stone Age existence, much as cavemen lived thousands of years ago in Britain. They make fire by spinning a hard, pointed stick between their hands into a hole made in a piece of softer wood; this produces a spark in about ten minutes. They make stone axes for splitting open hard fruits and stems, but do not use axes as weapons. Indeed, they have no word that means 'war'. The tribe are naked except for loin cloths and leaf skirts. Communication with the explorers was by means of several interpreters who translated first from Tasaday, which was understood imperfectly, into other languages before the reply was received in English.

The tribe live in caves gouged by nature from a cliff face. Vines and other vegetation cover the cave entrances. The tribesmen say that they have always lived in the caves, and that their ancestors had a 'good' dream which told them never to leave. The main cave is about 15 metres deep. Natural corners and shelves are used to store things. Lengths of bamboo are filled with water for drinking, and food is roasted over the fire. They eat wild yams, tadpoles, frogs, small fish, crabs, berries, and grubs found inside logs. Children urinate on the cave floor. Possessions are shared jointly, and everyone works towards the common good. Children are not punished by being struck. This tiny tribe of gentle people, probably one of the oldest living in such a way, indicates that primeval man was perhaps not the brutal creature that is so often imagined.

Ancient Homes

Much can be learned from primitive tribes today about the conditions under which early man lived thousands of years ago. In addition, early man has left traces of his habitations. Often these must have been permanent homes. The Tasadays prove that a tribe can live in one place, gathering the food necessary for survival from within a radius of a few miles. The general picture has always been of early man wandering continuously in order to find enough food to live. The Tasadays show that this idea is not necessarily sound.

The difficulty in studying the buildings of early man is twofold: first, there

1 Stonehenge consists of the remains of a number of prehistoric stone circles, situated on the Wiltshire Downs near Salisbury. Some stones were transported from the Prescelly Hills in Pembrokeshire, and sandstone blocks — each weighing as much as 50 tonnes — came from the Marlborough Downs. It seems likely that Stonehenge was used to keep a check on the calendar — the sun on midsummer morning rises behind the Heel Stone.

was tremendous variation in the structures themselves, both in period and area; and secondly the different periods of time into which historians slice up the 'prehistoric' era usually cover many thousands of years. Little remains of prehistoric buildings and, if anything is to be learned from the sites of ancient homes, they must be excavated by trained archaeologists. Modern archaeological methods can discover a great deal about such buildings, even when the original building materials have decayed. Rubble and rubbish that collected on the floor of a building give an indication of its size and shape. Wooden support posts, long since decayed, are shown by their holes which now stand out as black soil. The holes indicate whether the posts were thick or slender, how close together they were placed and whether they were positioned vertically or leaning inwards. Hearth-stones and ashes mark the position of a fire.

Prehistory can be divided into stages, corresponding to man's technical advance: the Palaeolithic, Mesolithic, Neolithic, Bronze and Iron Ages. In the next few pages we will look briefly at the principal building achievements of each phase.

The Palaeolithic Age

The common idea that man in the Palaeolithic or Old Stone Age invariably lived in caves is clearly false. Obviously he could only live in caves in areas where caves were to be found, and cave occupation was the exception not the rule. Caves did not make very comfortable homes, but at least they provided shelter from rain, extreme cold and wild beasts. There are probably many cave homes dating from Palaeolithic times still undiscovered — silent witnesses of an era long gone by, whose entrances are now blocked by fallen rocks or soil.

It is unusual to find caves which can definitely be said to have been used by Palaeolithic man. These people were hunters and would only resort to caves for casual shelter as the need arose. Evidence of occupation must therefore come from archaeological finds, worked flints for example, left behind by early man. These are difficult to spot and, in any case, are nearly always covered by deposits of cave rubbish from a later period. However a number of Palaeolithic cave dwellings have been identified, including some very large caves such as Kent's Cavern at Torquay, Gough's Cave in the Cheddar Gorge and Creswell Crags in Nottinghamshire.

A more widespread type of Palaeolithic find is discovered when the land is disturbed by quarrying or gravel digging. But on these open sites, implements such as axes are seldom found in the position in which they were left by Palaeolithic man — they have usually been carried some distance by the slow action of water. This means that true sites can only be recognized for certain in man-made sections cut through the ground. Such sites have been excavated in the Thames valley, Hampshire and East Anglia.

Early man in Britain lived mainly in the south and east of England. He avoided forests which harboured dangerous animals and were difficult to penetrate, and lived instead on hill slopes and sandy land. Very early homes have been excavated near Farnham in Surrey. These were hollows scooped out of gravel and then covered with thick branches, turf and other vegetation to make a roof.

Other simple structures must have been little more than windbreaks, much as people use today to protect themselves from a breeze while sunbathing on the beach. Frameworks of branches covered with leaves and grass could be joined together to form a simple covered ridge tent. These tents would have given a measure of protection during wet, windy or very cold weather, but they cannot have provided much shelter in winter when the nearby fire would have been the only way to keep warm. The fire also protected man from marauding beasts, which were frightened by the blaze, and enabled him to cook the meat of the animals he killed.

The Mesolithic Age

During the Mesolithic or Middle Stone Age, the weather in Britain began to get warmer. The polar ice caps melted and about 8,000 BC Britain became an island. The Mesolithic hunters and fishermen lived in small groups close to their food supplies. At Star Carr near Seamer in Yorkshire there was once a large lake where the Vale of Pickering is situated today. One site near there was buried in peat, which preserves wood and bone. Pollen analysis and Carbon 14 techniques have dated the site to about 8,000 BC, just after the last ice age. The hunters lived by the edge of the lake in simple huts built on a platform of birch trees which they felled for the purpose. They fished from dug-out canoes with harpoons and fish-hooks made out of bone. In contrast to these huts on a platform, a trench structure dating from about the same period has been found at Abinger in Surrey. The trench-like dwellings were cut into the rock.

Gradually man began to build his home beside others for companionship as well as for safety, and the first settlements grew up. Animals were tamed and fences made of stakes were put round the encampment to protect the animals and prevent them from straying. Encampments were made on upland hills and on the Downs, which provided good grazing for herds and flocks. Homes were still only simple structures, the bare minimum for shelter and sleeping. The most common consisted of long poles joined together at the top — like a Red Indian tent — and then filled in with woven branches and covered with leaves, vegetation, turf or clay.

The Neolithic Age

In the Neolithic or New Stone Age, men not only kept flocks and herds but also began to grow crops. Hoes were made out of flint, and antlers were used to make picks. Man became more settled and lived in larger groups. He began to realize that stone, in those areas where it was available, was a much longer-lasting material than branches, turf or skins. There was much local variation in the types of buildings erected. Round as well as rectangular houses have been found at Lough Gur in Ireland. In England, simple shallow pits have been uncovered, including one at Hurst Fen near Mildenhall in Suffolk. Haldon Hill near Exeter is the site of a timber building that once measured 6 by 4½ metres.

The small number of Neolithic houses found in Britain may be accounted for by the fact that most were built on chalk land. Erosion over the last 5,000 years has lowered the level of the surface chalk, so that any post holes in the upper layer of Neolithic chalk have been washed away.

Circular stone huts were built in areas where stone was plentiful. A large post in the centre of the hut supported the branch roof and this was covered with turf. The height of a hut could be increased by digging out the earth and lowering the level of the floor by as much as a metre.

Stone sites have been discovered in the Orkneys, north of Scotland, of which Skara Brae is the best-preserved. Local stone was used, split into long slabs. The settlement was later covered by sandstorms and has remained unweathered. The small settlement of stone houses, with rounded corners, was built about 1,500 BC. The largest houses were about 6 metres square. Doors were closed with stone slabs, and these could even be locked with stone bolts. Stone was also used to make furniture. The houses were almost circular and each consisted of one room. There were also alcoves, probably used as places to store things and as privies. The smoke from the peat fire in the centre of the room escaped through a hole in the roof. Beds were made of a box frame of stone, filled with heather to make a springy mattress. There were stone cupboards for storage; and a stone canopy over the bed could be covered with skins to give privacy and protection from draughts.

Field Monuments

No monuments, as distinct from houses, dating from the earlier prehistoric ages have been found, but these were common by the Neolithic phase which began in Britain about 6,000 years ago. Once life became safer and less of a struggle against the elements man was able to think of building monuments. Usually these had a religious significance.

Long barrows were one of the earliest field monuments in Britain. These were burial places for large numbers of people. Some may have been family graves, and sometimes as many as 50 people were buried in one barrow. In areas where there was no stone, they were made of rubble and earth. Generally they were about 45 metres long and nearly 2 metres high at the higher end. Most long barrows are found in the south of England.

Chambered long barrows were also used for mass burial. These included an entrance passage, so that additional burials could take place at a later date. However, the entrance passage meant that they were easier for treasure-seekers to get into, and many were plundered over the centuries. The barrows were covered by a mound of stones, and the stones were often later removed to build roads and walls. The monuments that remain are known as cromlechs in Wales and as dolmens elsewhere, including Cornwall. There are many chambered long barrows in the south of England from the Mendips to the Cotswolds.

Camps encircled by causeways have been discovered in Wessex and other southern areas, particularly on Salisbury Plain. Windmill Hill, north of Avebury, was the first to be systematically excavated. These camps consist of up to three rings of banks and ditches. Each ring is well separated from the others. At first glance they would appear to have been designed for defensive purposes, but there is no real evidence of an internal structure. Another view is that they were cattle corrals, as many bones have been unearthed. But it seems most likely that the causewayed camps were places for periodic feasts — a kind of prehistoric religious fairground. This would explain the numbers of

2 Remains of prehistoric buildings at Jarlshof in Shetland.

3 (*Below*) A stone fort near Londonderry.

4 A model of a reconstructed Iron Age farmstead.

concentric rings: when the population grew Neolithic man needed to extend the area for this social gathering by building another earth bank to form the new outer boundary. Causewayed camps are difficult if not almost impossible to spot from ground level, and aerial photography is likely to yield the most rewarding finds in the future.

Another form of Neolithic structure was the cursus — a pair of long earth banks about 90 metres apart, running parallel usually for about 3 kilometres, although one in Dorset is 9.6 kilometres long. They appear to have been used for games — hence their name 'cursus' which is the Latin for 'racecourse'.

Probably the best-known of the Neolithic field structures are the various forms of henge monuments: Stonehenge and Avebury, for instance. More than 60 henge monuments have now been discovered in Britain. Some sites have upright stones only; others, such as Stonehenge, include lintel stones that hang or rest on the uprights. A number of these monuments were made of wood, and Woodhenge, 3 kilometres from Stonehenge, was discovered from the air.

Most henge monuments are almost circular, with diameters ranging from only 9 metres to as much as 480 metres. They have been discovered in England, Scotland and Wales. Most of them are near a burial place, which indicates perhaps that they were used for some religious purpose. In fact, Stonehenge itself is surrounded by the largest collection of barrows in Britain. There are also stone circles inside henges and free-standing circles such as the one in Cumberland known as 'Long Meg and her Daughters'.

Round barrows are very common, and more than 20,000 of them have been found in Britain. Most belong to the Bronze Age (which followed the Neolithic Age), between 2,000 and 500 BC. The term 'tumuli' is often used to describe these burial mounds.

The variety, dimensions, distribution and numbers of prehistoric field monuments indicate that, by the Neolithic Age, man was able to conceive and build huge constructions, following co-ordinated plans. He was now by no means the primitive creature that his ancestors had been.

The Bronze Age

There have been many finds of bronze weapons and tools in Britain, but buildings dating from the Bronze Age are much more difficult to discover. It would seem, however, that most of the buildings were round. Remains of farmhouses have been identified with rectangular fields nearby for growing crops.

On Dartmoor there were large circular enclosures — called pounds — perhaps 30 metres in diameter, surrounded by a stone wall. Inside the enclosure were small circular huts with dry stone walls. Grimspound is a good example of this type of settlement.

The Iron Age

Most settlements in the Iron Age, after 500 BC, consisted of a farm, an enclosed area surrounding it and a field system. Some were grouped to form tiny hamlets of about six units. In places where wood was still used for houses, little trace of them remains today. Huts made of stone had a much better chance of survival, particularly if situated in remote countryside where stone robbing was impractical. Many such hamlets have been found in Wales, Cornwall and Northumberland.

The use of more sophisticated tools in the Iron Age allowed man to fell larger trees. Huge beams were used to make some of the bigger houses. The remains of a circular building at Little Woodbury in Wiltshire show that the building was 15 metres across. It had thick posts round the perimeter and four more in the centre to support the roof. Clearly this was the house of a wealthy farmer.

A very different form of wooden building has been discovered in two villages in Somerset. At Glastonbury and Meare — formerly on the shore of a large lake — platforms of earth and stone were built on piles driven into the lake, and then wooden houses were erected on the platforms. The Glastonbury

13

settlement held a large number of inhabitants, and the marshy flooded area surrounding the settlement gave protection against attack. About 60 houses were built on the platform and the settlement was enclosed by a wooden stockade. The circular buildings measured about 6 metres across. The wall posts were filled in with branches and clay, and the roof was thatched with reeds. Because of the damp nature of the site, much material has been preserved that would not normally survive in a dry area. The tools and well-made household utensils show how advanced these people were. A similar site has been excavated in marshland at Skipsea in Yorkshire.

In view of the tribal nature of the times, it is hardly surprising that so many defensive structures have been unearthed. Hill-forts were important means of defence. Some had only a few huts but others contained many buildings, as at Maiden Castle and Hod Hill in Dorset. Almost all hill-forts were built on high land and had at least a single outer earth bank; many had multiple banks. The archaeologist tries to determine from the grassy banks he sees today what the hill-fort originally looked like. Some hill-forts can only be recognized now in photographs taken from the air. Woodbury near Salisbury, for instance, was identified in this way because of its large bank; on excavation, the ditch was found to be more than 4 metres deep.

Hill-forts have been discovered in many parts of Britain, particularly in Wessex, the Welsh Marches, Wiltshire and the South Downs. But they are rare in Norfolk and Suffolk, and places north of the Humber. Iron Age man often chose his sites so well that they were later re-used in medieval times, as happened at British Camp in the Malvern Hills. At Old Sarum near Salisbury, a Norman castle and cathedral and also part of a medieval town were all sited inside the area of an Iron Age fort. Similarly, Stirling Castle and Edinburgh Castle were built on the sites of old forts.

5 Iron Age wattle and daub huts, reconstructed in a folk park.

6 (*Opposite*) The remains of part of Hadrian's Wall, at Borcovicium, in the Northumberland countryside.

2. Roman Britain

The Romans in Britain

In the story of house-building the prehistoric phase in British history is most naturally followed by the activities of the Saxon builders. The period of Roman occupation saw an insertion of new ideas imported from abroad, which halted the general continuity of simple building techniques for some 400 years.

Julius Caesar's first exploratory expedition to Britain took place in 55 BC. During the following century contact with Rome increased, trading posts were set up and luxury goods and wine were imported to Britain. In AD 43 came the invasion of Claudius, which made Rome master of much of lowland Britain and superimposed a foreign culture and superior standards on the Britons. But Britain was difficult to invade and even more difficult to keep under subjection. There were villages remote in clearings in the forests and on the hills. Valleys, marshes, rivers and forests made much of Britain inaccessible and difficult to supervise. Celtic tribes on the Scottish borders, in Wales and in Cornwall were largely unaffected by Roman rule, and continued to live much as before. To keep the tribes at bay, Scotland was walled-off by Hadrian's Wall, running for about 117 kilometres from the Solway Firth to Wallsend. Hadrian's Wall was nearly 3 metres wide, and 4 to 5 metres high. There was a deep trench on the north side of the wall, and forts were built along the wall itself.

In Roman Britain as a whole, there was much emphasis on military building. Legionary fortresses, for example, were built as a base for the legions when not on campaign. The fortresses were rectangular with four main gates. The principal ones were at York, Chester and Caerleon (in South Wales) but there were others at Lincoln, Gloucester and Inchtuthil in Perthshire. A civilian settlement usually sprang up quickly near a fortress. There were also many forts, similar to the fortresses, but smaller. Those housing cavalry units were generally larger than the ones for infantry units. The Roman influence was most strongly felt in lowland Britain — south and east England especially.

Roads were constructed all over the country, along which troops moved quickly and efficiently. Forts and towns were built to various patterns with a regular grid, and the Romans organized an efficient water supply as well as paved streets and drainage. In addition to well-built houses there were shops and public buildings such as baths, temples, arenas and town halls. Large houses — villas — were built in the countryside. Although these new buildings were at first intended only for Roman officials and merchants, it was not long before wealthy Britons began to copy them. They too wanted comfort.

Towns

King George VI, father of Queen Elizabeth II, declared on receiving the Freedom of the City of York that the history of York is the history of England. There are two senses in which this statement is true, not only of York but of most ancient cities. First, many old cities have played a part in

7 Detail from a Roman mosaic at Chedworth Villa in Gloucestershire. Many interior mosaic pavements were decorated with mythological figures and complicated patterns.

shaping the history of Britain because of the events which happened there over the centuries; and secondly, ancient cities often still show traces of man's habitation from pre-Roman times up to the present day. There are many towns which today have pre-Roman or Roman remains to remind us that there have been continuous settlements on these sites for at least 2,000 years.

In building, the Romans used imported as well as native stone, and also brick, tile and concrete. The use of these latter materials was an innovation in Britain. Many Roman buildings consisted of thick foundations of stone on which rested a timber construction. Others were made of wood. Archaeologists, however, must often be satisfied with the discovery of the trenches in which the Roman walls once stood. In most cases the walls themselves have long since been removed, leaving only wall-footings. Yet the outline of a Roman building can be accurately pieced together from such finds. There may be a great deal of scatter such as rubble, roof tiles, plaster, nails, pieces of pottery, coins, black soil, bones and shells — the Romans were very fond of oysters and piles of shells are often found on digs. Deep ploughing on arable land can frequently produce finds. Or else moles and rabbits on grassland may throw scatter to the surface, and in dry weather a promising site may show as a parched area, indicating the possibility of shallow soil on top of buried foundations. Aerial photography is a great help in recognizing such sites.

Town houses for the wealthy Romans were splendid buildings, consisting of a courtyard open to the sky and surrounded by rooms. Some even had a library and a chapel. The houses were centrally heated by a hypocaust — the floor rested on short pillars and warm air from a stoke hole was fed under the floor. The heating even extended to the walls where box (or hollow) tiles were fixed to allow warm air to rise inside the walls.

The interior walls of houses belonging to the wealthy were often plastered over and decorated with brightly painted scenes. The floors were made of thousands of small coloured stones. These mosaics — a sort of stone carpet — were set in cement and formed intricate patterns and pictures.

Slaves or ordinary working people in towns often lived in blocks of flats, made of brick and sometimes four storeys high.

Villas

Vitruvius was a Roman architect who published ten books on architecture. He wrote about the types of houses that were suitable for various ranks of people. There were standard shapes and fixed proportions for buildings. About villas in the country he wrote:

> They should be dependent on the extent of the land attached to them, and its produce. The courts and their dimensions will be determined by the number of cattle, and the yokes of oxen employed . . . If villas are required to be erected of more magnificence than ordinary, they must be formed according to the properties laid down for town houses.

The remains of hundreds of villas have been unearthed in many parts of Roman Britain. A villa was a large country house belonging to a wealthy landowner, surrounded by a farm and containing sheds, stables and simple living accommodation for the estate workers. Villas usually had brick or thick concrete walls, with an upper storey made from a timber frame filled in with wicker and daub. There was often a courtyard enclosed on three sides by a corridor. Window glass — generally in the form of small greeny-blue panes — was set in wooden or metal frames. Like the town houses of the wealthy, villas had painted interior walls and mosaic pavements on the floors of the main rooms. Some rooms were heated by a hypocaust. Villas were well furnished with tables, chairs, couches and beds, mostly made of wood. Archaeology has revealed a wealth of household utensils ranging from candlesticks and sculpture to pottery and nutcrackers. Each villa had a staff of servants. Some villas seem to have been suburban rather than rural and were therefore partly dependent on a nearby town for produce. Villas of this type were usually owned by merchant-farmers, whose first interest was town trade rather than farming.

Although villas were magnificent buildings for the wealthy, the peasants who cultivated the land around the villa lived in simple wattle and daub houses or even in pit huts. There can have been little chance for them to enjoy the comfort of their masters.

8 A reconstructed drawing of a Roman villa at Lullingstone in Kent. The villa's wealthy owner employed many servants and farmed the surrounding land. The walls were decorated with Christian wall-paintings and there were intricate mosaic patterns on the floors of the main rooms.

3. Saxons and Normans

Saxon Halls

The Britain that was abandoned by the Romans in AD 410 was a land of thick forest, with small clearings made by man for ploughing and animal grazing. The Romans, themselves invaders, left a land open to attack; and after their withdrawal in 410, the Britons were pushed further and further westwards into wilder and more inaccessible areas — into Ireland, Wales and the West Country — following each successive wave of conquerors from the mainland of Europe. The Picts invaded England from Scotland and Saxons crossed the sea and settled in the south and east of the country. The Saxons looted the towns but then avoided them, choosing instead to make and live in their own forest clearings. They built timber-framed houses and defended them with stockades and ditches. Roman towns and villas fell into ruins. Occasionally, building materials from these towns were stolen as happened at St Alban's Abbey where, towards the end of the Saxon era, bricks from the Roman city of Verulamium were used to build the abbey's square tower.

The Saxon church at Bradford-on-Avon in Wiltshire survives to show that the Saxons knew how to build fine buildings from stone. But for much of the Saxon period there was little building with either brick or stone. The settlers were usually content to clear a small part of the forest, construct simple wooden houses and set about growing crops and rearing animals. Town life diminished. The Saxon settlement was rural and agricultural, based round a hall for the chief, smaller huts or houses for the tribesmen, and a wooden stockade to give protection from attack. Because of the numerous different tribes living in Britain at this time, there was constant unease and frequent skirmishes; as a result most buildings were put up with an eye to defence.

9 (*Opposite*) The impregnable keep at Castle Hedingham in Essex.

10 (*Right*) A cruck house (on the right) near Tewkesbury in Gloucestershire. For many centuries curved end timbers were called crucks; they were the split halves of tree trunks and were used to support the structure.

Water meadows — or hams — on the eastern river valleys were needed to give pasture and meadow, resulting in such settlements as Gillingham, Framlingham and so on. Similarly, settlers cleared patches of forest — making a feld — in the Weald of Kent. Henfield and Lingfield, for instance, were settlements cleared in this way from the forest. The Saxon farmhouse was simple in plan, similar to a large barn, housing both people and cattle under one roof. The family lived and slept at one end and there was a hearth in the centre, while the animals were stalled at the other end of the building. The earliest structures had a row of posts down the middle to support the roof.

The Saxons were a seafaring people, and their expert shipwrights advised on building construction. The forester would select trees that bent so that part sloped away from the upright. This formed a pointed arch at each side of the house, which was joined at the top to support the roof ridge. These frameworks were called 'crucks' and became common in the north and the Midlands. The wooden upright posts that had previously supported the roof could now be dispensed with, since the roof was supported on the timber arch at each side of the house. This made the interior of the hall seem much more spacious and attractive. A large hall now looked really large.

As the number of people living in a settlement increased, it became more and more difficult to fit everyone inside the main farmhouse — especially at meal-times — so cattle were gradually relegated to out-buildings.

An open hearth in the centre of the floor heated the hall and was used for cooking. A hole in the thatched roof allowed smoke to escape. These holes were sometimes quite large, and on at least one occasion a man managed to escape through one. The story tells how King Olaf Trygvesson, tired of the sorcerers' tricks, invited them to a party, got them drunk and then set the house on fire. To the king's fury, one sorcerer succeeded in climbing through the smoke-hole, and escaped over the roof.

Upper storeys were later constructed by laying floor boards along the beams. Access was by an external staircase or, more simply, by an internal ladder. The upper floor provided a useful sleeping space, and a welcome escape from the appallingly cramped living conditions, the smoke, rain and draughts. A building with an upper storey could not have a central fire, so the fire was now built in a side wall, with a cover of stone or plastered timber through which smoke escaped to the roof.

Other houses were constructed from a pointed arch of timber, with the roof resting on the ground. One such house, dating from a later period, still exists at Scrivelsby in Lincolnshire. It is called Teapot Hall, which has led to the saying:

Teapot Hall,
All roof, no wall.

It has one large living space and a bedroom upstairs. Some Viking huts were similar in design.

The remains of wooden buildings dating from the early seventh century have been excavated at Yeavering near Wooler in Northumberland. The site, located from the air, was once a royal residence with a large hall, a Christian church, a pagan shrine and a large building for assemblies. The latter was copied from part of a Roman amphitheatre. A tenth-century royal manor, residence of the Kings of Wessex, has been excavated at Cheddar in Somerset. Among the largest of its timber buildings was a hall with a roof span of 18 metres.

The houses for the ordinary farm-workers were simple in the extreme. No Saxon or Norman timber houses remain in Britain but there are two-storey stone houses dating from the end of the twelfth century, as at Portslade near Brighton and Hemingford Grey near Huntingdon. The larger stone-built halls looked like the nave of a small church. Magnificent halls were built at Winchester and Westminster in the early twelfth century, but these were places where government was carried on and bore almost no resemblance to the ordinary type of structure.

Towns were small in Saxon times and had surrounding walls to protect the citizens from attack, while halls in the countryside relied on wooden stockades.

Norman Castles

England was conquered again in 1066 when William, Duke of Normandy, claimed that he had been nominated to succeed to the throne by Edward the Confessor. The country was shared out between the Norman lords who had made up William's attacking force, and castles were built at all strategic points.

The earliest castles were made of wood, later to be replaced by stone. An artificial mound (as at Clifford's Tower at York) was often erected as a site for a castle, which was usually built where it could most easily be defended. A wooden castle was then constructed on top of this mound, and a fenced courtyard, called a bailey, surrounded it.

Pictures of buildings on the Bayeux Tapestry are portrayed in the same conventional way as on the manuscripts of the period. Houses seem usually to have had two storeys. Prominence was given on the tapestry to the new Abbey at Westminster, and castles were shown as a mound with a stockade on top, the whole being surrounded by a moat. The timbers supporting the stockade were probably embedded deep in the ground, sometimes even under the earth mound itself.

Castles were built in most towns where a regular market was held, so providing security for townsfolk and visitors as well as an ever-present sign of Norman dominance. Castles built in the countryside seem to have survived better than those built in towns. The Channel ports were protected, and a chain of castles in South Wales defended the Vale of Glamorgan against attack from the Welsh.

The main building inside the castle walls was the keep — a rectangular or circular tower, usually four storeys high. This contained a chapel, kitchens, an armoury, storerooms and a large communal hall. Cellars and dungeons were built below ground level. Spiral stairs were set into the walls, which were often up to 4½ metres thick. Local stone was used where possible, but stone for building was also imported from Caen in Normandy.

There could have been little comfort for anyone in an early castle but, as times became safer, tapestries were hung on interior walls, windows were closed with wooden shutters, and rushes and straw were spread over the floor. Larger castles had a solar, a room where the lord could retire in private, away from the busy atmosphere of the great hall.

At first there was a fire in the centre of the hall, but from the twelfth century this began to be moved into a wall. The smoke was carried upwards inside the wall and escaped through a hole a short distance away. On windy days, however, the smoke would often blow down the hole and into the hall.

A moat was built round the castle to give added protection. Often these were wet ditches, but sometimes large dry ditches were constructed to hinder the approach of an enemy. Yet, despite wall-mining, battering-rams, siege-towers and huge slings for propelling boulders, few castles seemed to fall to their attackers. Before the days of gunpowder — which effectively meant the end of castles as defensive homes — castles under siege were much more likely to fall to the enemy through internal disloyalty or famine than through successful attacking tactics.

Castles continued to be built throughout the Middle Ages. Huge castles

A large hall, dating from the thirteenth century, at Stokesay Castle in Shropshire.

remain in Wales, some with several curtain walls, and towers built to defend the keep from any direction. The architects and castle builders were learning a great deal about stone masonry, and this knowledge was put to good use in the building of ordinary homes for wealthy citizens who did not need the massive defence of a castle.

4. Medieval Builders

13 (*Above*) Medieval timber houses at Stratford-on-Avon in Warwickshire. The upper storeys project outwards on all sides.

14 (*Right*) The banqueting hall of a rich wool merchant at Salisbury, built about 1470.

Manor Houses

Early Norman manor houses often looked as if they had been built more for defence than as a comfortable home, with stone walls and even a moat surrounding the house. The hall was usually built on the first floor — and was approached by an external stairway. The room on the ground floor — known as the undercroft — was used for storage. Little Wenham Hall in Suffolk is a typical manor house, built of brick in the mid-thirteenth century. From the twelfth century onwards some manor houses had the hall on the ground floor. A solar was added at one end of the house to provide privacy for the lord and his family. This was often an upstairs room reached by an internal staircase or by a ladder or staircase added outside. Penshurst Place in Kent, built by a London merchant, shows that by the fourteenth century manor houses had become more pleasant places in which to live. They were lighted with pointed Gothic windows, and were less draughty and much more comfortable than the earlier Norman buildings. The tall pointed windows were similar to those found in churches. In fact, both churches and manor houses were built by the same architects and masons, using much the same methods. By the fifteenth century a section had been added at each end of the manor house, making three parts in all. Because of the central hall's high roof, there was no direct access between the end buildings.

Throughout the Middle Ages it was usual for the manor house to be made of timber, filled in with wattle and daub panels. Woven branches (wattle) were placed between the main posts, and over this clay was daubed and left to dry.

The great hall remained the central meeting-place where most of the people lived, slept and ate. The lord and his family often dined on a raised dais at one end of the hall, separated from the rest of the household. In his absence, the lord could keep an eye on the activities in the hall from his own private apartment. At Penshurst Place there is a slit in the wall of the solar; and at Great Chalfield in Wiltshire — built in the fifteenth century — hollow eyes in the stone heads high on the wall in the great hall serve as perfect peep-holes.

Medieval Towns

Medieval towns were small and often surrounded by stone walls. Streets were usually only 2 or 3 metres wide — as at the Shambles in York — and houses were built close together to save space. Party walls joining two houses together were supposed to be about a metre thick and made of stone, for fire was a constant threat in medieval towns. Houses were built upwards by adding one or even two storeys above the first floor. By the fifteenth century, manor houses and town houses were either entirely stone-built or even still made of timber and wattle.

The Paston family, who lived in the fifteenth century, are well-known for their letters which have survived to this day. One such letter shows that a storey — from floor to ceiling — in a medieval house was far from high. Margaret Paston wrote from Norfolk to her husband in London: 'Get some crossbows . . . for your houses here be so low that there may be none man shoot out with a long bow, though we had never so much need.'

At first the only people who needed special protection were the wealthy who built stone houses in towns. The Jews' House at Lincoln, for instance, which still survives, was built in 1150. As Jews at that time were money-lenders, and not always popular with the people to whom they lent money at interest, they may have felt safer inside a stone house. Simple timber and wattle houses were far from secure dwellings — thieves could enter easily through the thin walls, and one man was even murdered while sitting at home by an assailant who stuck a spear through the wall of his house!

London has had ten disastrous fires in its history, the first in 961 and the last in 1940. The Assise of Buildings in 1212 — the year of the seventh fire — stated that 'in ancient times the greater part of the city was built of wood, and the houses were covered with straw and stubble and the like.' An ordinance passed in the same year, 1212, decreed that all thatched roofs in London should be whitewashed and cookshops plastered both inside and out. Stone buildings were also very often erected in an attempt to stop fires from spreading. This was a difficult problem in the days of open fireplaces, candles and flaring torches, but some success was achieved; since 1212 only three major fires have ravaged the city: in 1264, 1666 and the Blitz of 1940.

The change-over from timber to stone houses was a gradual process and not always constant. Building in stone was expensive and the stone itself was difficult to obtain in areas that had no natural supply. However, when houses became taller with the addition of new floors, this created problems for the architect-builder. The problems were easily solved in the case of stone-built houses, because the party walls could be heightened and floors were simply inserted where they were needed. It was a different matter when it came to building three- or four-storey houses with timber. If too much pressure was exerted on the floor the floorboards would bounce up and down, even when just a few people walked across the room, and this movement then spread to other storeys. The difficulty was solved by using longer and longer planks for each successive storey, which resulted in the overhanging floor or 'jetty'. This stabilized the building, but created an unusual shape. Buildings that stood alone, such as a guildhall, might have jetties on four sides, making a very top-heavy erection.

The living conditions of the peasantry were not improving at anything like the rate of the housing built for the wealthy. Most peasants, as well as artisans in the towns, lived in broken-down hovels. The floor was bare stamped earth, on top of which a fire was laid. The smoke escaped in all directions and people lived in a 'ful sooty' atmosphere of filth and dirt. Streets of badly-made houses

15 Goodramgate in York has half-timbered buildings with overhanging upper storeys. The central tower of York Minster is in the centre of this picture, with the twin towers at the west end. The tower on the far left is Holy Trinity, Goodramgate, a medieval church with box pews and a very uneven pavement.

were termed Rotten Row, and there were certainly many of these.

In some parts of the country, even in the fifteenth century, houses were still being built as strongholds — with narrow windows well above the ground and thick walls. This was particularly the case along the Welsh border, and in the northern counties of Durham, Northumberland, Westmorland, Cumberland and even in north Yorkshire.

Buildings Bought with Wool

Wool was the most productive crop in the later Middle Ages and profits from its sale were used to erect magnificent stone houses in villages, as at Chipping Campden in Gloucestershire. Such places as Lavenham in Suffolk. benefited from the trade in cloth. The export of wool from England to the continent increased greatly during the fourteenth century, and at times countries in Europe were hard put to send enough commodities to England to balance the trading books. Wine was England's main import, and those countries that did not produce wine often had to send ships to England carrying ballast in order to fill their holds with wool on the return journey. Bricks were also often brought over and sold. This was the origin of most of the brick buildings in East Anglia.

In the mid-fourteenth century England was struck by the Black Death, a plague which killed about one third of the country's population. Crops rotted in fields with no-one to tend them and labour, unorganized as it was, could demand and receive higher wages than before. Conditions became desperate.

Many landowners turned to sheep-rearing as an easier alternative to crop-growing. Sheep required relatively little tending. They roamed freely and fed themselves. Moreover, their wool commanded high prices. The lush pasture land available in England made the country the envy of war-torn Europe, where invading armies had decimated flocks for mutton.

Landowners grew rich on the profits from wool and many improved their material comforts and rebuilt their houses in grander styles. Windows became larger as round Norman arches gave way to the pointed arch. Glass, however, was still expensive. If it was used at all it was fixed in a frame, and the frame was then fitted into the window opening. Only the lower part — the casement — opened to let in fresh air, and the whole frame was taken away as part of the furniture when the owner moved house. Interior walls were sometimes plastered by using burned chalk or powdered limestone mixed with hair or straw and water, and the plaster was painted over.

The basic building plan remained simple and much as before. A house was made from a framework of thick wooden beams. These supported the roof and the various floors. The walls between the beams were covered in with stone rubble and then plastered. The external beams formed part of the decoration of the house and were not plastered. The roof was tiled with clay or stone. But fashions change, and in the Tudor age Britain became a land of brick-built houses, except in those parts of the country where natural stone was easily found.

Churches and Cathedrals

Even counting every surviving medieval house, great hall, palace, guildhall and the occasional shop and school, these buildings appear few in number when compared with the hundreds of medieval churches that still exist today. A medieval town such as York boasted about 50 churches — almost one for every week of the year — but sadly of these less than 20 still survive, and some of them are unused.

Few churches display a single style of architecture which would date the building to a specific period. The Saxon church of St Lawrence at Bradford-on-Avon is one exception, as is the Norman church at Barfreston in Kent. But most medieval churches were built over a long period — with additions of a chapel, an aisle or a tower — and this is reflected in the differing styles that were used.

In the twelfth century — and for long after — the parish church was in a very real sense a centre of communal life, not simply a building where services were held. The nave of the church was used by the congregation as a sort of village hall. During services the congregation knelt or stood on the stone floor. There were no rows of wooden pews as there are today, and so stone seats were provided for the elderly and sick. These were built round the wall of the nave,

16 Part of the cloisters at Wells Cathedral. Cloisters ran along four sides of an open quadrangle; they were used for walking and in many monasteries the monks also worked in them, sitting at small desks in narrow cells called carrels.

hence the expression 'the weakest go to the wall'.

Early churches were, of course, made of wood, which was only gradually replaced by stone. In time, most churches and also cathedrals — the regional seats of bishops — were constructed in the shape of a cross, with the altar at the east end. Westminster Abbey, built by Edward the Confessor (1042-66), was the first such cruciform church in England. This is how a contemporary described the building:

17 The choir of York Minster, one of the largest medieval cathedrals in England. The choir was begun in 1361, and was built round the Norman portion of the church. The great east window contains 153 large panels and over 250 small ones.

Now he laid the foundations of the church
With large square blocks of grey stone.
Its foundations are deep,
The front, towards the east he makes round,
The stones are very strong and hard.
In the centre rises a tower
And two at the western front,
And fine and large bells he hangs there.
The pillars and mouldings
Are rich without and within.
At the basis and the capitals
The work rises grand and royal.

Sculptured are the stones
And storied the windows.
All are made with the skill
Of good and loyal workmanship.
And when he finished the work
He covers the church with lead.

Monasteries

Since the seventh century or even before, men who wanted to lead a life away from the world, in prayer and communal living, had formed communities of monks. Cells were established on Iona off the west coast of Scotland by Celtic missionaries from Ireland in AD 563. Monasticism later spread to England, and the Holy Island of Lindisfarne was the site of one of the first monasteries in England. The earliest monastic buildings were made of wood and, of course, were easily destroyed; in time, they gave way to more substantial buildings in stone. After 1066, the Normans injected fresh enthusiasm into the monastic ideal and financed many new monasteries as well as rebuilding old ones.

Benedictine abbeys were usually built in towns where the monks could teach, heal, and help foster community spirit, while at the same time living a life apart and practising the three cardinal rules of poverty, celibacy and obedience. Through the centuries, various groups of monks became dissatisfied as the strict discipline was relaxed, and broke away to found new orders. One such group, the Cistercians, began to build their abbeys in the countryside, well away from the worldly influence of the towns. By good management and hard work, the Cistercian monks became some of the country's most successful rearers of sheep and sellers of wool.

The simple wooden monastery buildings were gradually replaced by stone ones, and many ruins remain today to show the extent of the planning and expertise needed to erect such large undertakings, often miles from the nearest town. The remoteness of Cistercian abbeys has spared many of them from the ravages of man, if not from time, whereas most Benedictine monasteries in the towns have long since been pillaged and destroyed for their stone or to make way for fresh buildings.

Except for the Carthusian order, where each monk lived most of his life in his own small cell with a walled garden behind it, the layout of most abbeys is very alike. The large church where the monks spent many hours each day was built on the north side of the cloisters, to protect the other monastic buildings from the north winds. Dining-room, chapter house, dormitory, infirmary, guest-house and abbot's dwelling were positioned around the central area, the whole forming in miniature a community that was to a large extent self-supporting. The building of these magnificent structures must have taxed the energies of some of the best architect-masons in the land.

18 Wells Cathedral in Somerset. Wells was a non-monastic cathedral, administered by secular canons, not by monks.

Medieval Architects

The working drawings of a few medieval architects have survived from about 1200 onwards although most drawings have long since been lost. Once used, the drawings were usually either discarded or destroyed, perhaps deliberately so. Many of the medieval guilds had their trade secrets, and the builders were certainly no exception. The number of pattern books and technical texts on building methods increased after about 1500, but the exact means by which processes were carried out remained obscure. Secrecy about building skills was common, and the following tale shows the value which masons placed on their secrets. In 1099, the Bishop of Utrecht ordered the building of a church to St Mary. Inadvertently, the master mason's son divulged to the bishop the secret of keeping water from the foundations. When the master mason found out that the bishop knew the secret, he grabbed a knife and stabbed him to death.

In England, from the sixteenth century, a scale model in wood was generally made of a projected building. This showed in miniature what the finished work would look like, and was also useful as a guide when estimating quantities and costs. Sir Christopher Wren's model for St Paul's Cathedral is perhaps the most famous of a number of models that have survived.

For medieval architects, practical building skills were as important as creative flair. They served an apprenticeship of about seven years, learning manual skills and acquiring the technical expertise required to erect a building and to supervise the operation from the laying of the first stone through to completion.

5. Tudor Buildings

19 Little Moreton Hall in Cheshire
is a fine example of Elizabethan
architecture, restored and administered by the National Trust.

Cottages

The antiquarian John Leyland travelled extensively in England between 1533 and 1544. In his description of the countryside he mentions many abandoned castles, dilapidated town walls and ruined monasteries. The latter were the result of the dissolution of the monastic houses by Henry VIII, beginning in the year 1536. Leyland almost certainly also saw many mean and ruined cottages belonging to poor villagers. However, in the years that followed, he would have noticed a resurgence in the building of homes for ordinary tenants and a definite improvement in comfort and structural soundness. Many cottages now had two storeys, with a good weather-proof roof, and boasted several rooms. They also had a fireplace with a chimney, and there might even be a loft — sometimes used as an extra bedroom — just below the roof. Access was by means of a ladder, in much the same way as people nowadays reach their loft. Some cottages were built of stone in the Cotswolds, Yorkshire and Cornwall, but in other areas they were still built of timber and plaster or, more unusually, of timber and brick.

The really poor, however — as in any age — saw little improvement. They continued to live in tiny one-room hovels, often still sharing accommodation with their animals. Their lot was hard; but life was even harsher for the peasants who lost jobs and homes as a result of the continuing change from arable to sheep farming. Henry VIII's edict of 1533, specifying that no-one was to own more than 2,000 sheep, seems to have had hardly any effect. The displaced peasants had little alternative but to become wanderers and beggars, and after 1536 there were no longer monasteries to provide succour to the vagrant in his misery. More serious still was the disendowment of monastic hospitals, which had provided a vital service for the destitute in the towns. About 1550, Crowley in his *Epigrams* described a conversation he heard between two beggars:

> They had both sore legs most loathsome to see,
> All raw from the foot well most to the knee.
> 'My leg,' quoth the one, 'I thank God is fair.'
> 'So is mine,' quoth the other,' in a cold air,
> For then it looketh raw and as red as any blood,
> I would not have it healed for any world's good.
> No man would pity me but for my sore leg,
> Wherefore if I were whole I might in vain beg.'

Tudor Homes

Peace had returned to England in 1485 with the end of the Wars of the Roses, a conflict which lasted 30 years and ruined many fortunes. Under the new strong Tudor government people, no longer afraid of wars and turmoil, began to have

20 A sixteenth-century moated manor at Gedding in Suffolk. Notice the fine brickwork.

the necessary confidence to build ambitious dwellings for themselves and their families.

Flanders supplied the earliest bricks to East Anglia, but from the fifteenth century bricks were manufactured in England. Depleted supplies of timber and the desire for chimneys together led to an increase in the number of buildings made of brick. Most bricks were red, but some were well burned, becoming dark blue. These vitreous bricks were used by the bricklayer to make patterns in the walls as, for instance, in the sixteenth-century parts of Hampton Court Palace, built by Cardinal Wolsey, and one of the best brick buildings from the Tudor age.

Half-timbered houses were also built during the sixteenth century. They were called this because they had a timber framework and the space between the timber beams was filled with narrow bricks. The wooden beams were fixed together with wooden pegs, since iron nails did not last in oak. As in the past, the upper storey was wider than the lower, resulting in a dark room downstairs and a bigger one above it.

The design of chimneys was often ornate and extravagant. Clay, tiles or slate began to be used instead of thatch for the roof. The fireplace, built outwards at the end of the living-room, provided space to sit at the sides of the fire. This was known as an 'inglenook'.

The ladder leading to the first floor was now replaced by a proper staircase, even if this was just a block of wood with notches cut into it to serve as steps. Some houses had a spiral staircase to save space. Interior walls were often

37

covered with carved wooden panels to cover the holes between the infilling and to keep out damp and draughts.

Towns grew so quickly in the Tudor age that buildings spread far beyond the town walls. The growth of London had been phenomenal, and in 1580 Queen Elizabeth issued a proclamation about the congested and insanitary conditions in the city:

> there are such great multitudes of people brought to inhabit in small rooms, whereof a great part are seen very poor, yea, such as must live of begging, or by worse means, and they heaped up together, and in a sort smothered by many families of children and servants in one house or small tenement; it must needs follow, if any plague or unpopular sickness should, by God's permission, enter amongst those multitudes, that the same would not only spread itself, and invade the whole city and confines, but that a great mortality would ensue . . . the infection would be also dispersed through all other parts of the realm, to the manifest danger of the whole body thereof.

The queen's forecast was proved tragically correct in 1665, when pestilence swept through the city, leaving scarcely a person untouched.

By an ordinance of 1592, new houses were forbidden within three miles of London, and no more than one family was allowed to inhabit any one house. Of course, this law was openly evaded and London, like all other cities, continued to grow apace.

Grand Mansions

Huge houses standing in private parks were built in the Tudor age by the very wealthy. A new class of well-off men was emerging, men made rich by trade, some of whom bought former monastic land as the sites for their new homes. At first, mansions were built around a courtyard, as at Longleat in Wiltshire, but in Elizabeth I's reign the main aim of architects was to create symmetry in the design. The external view of a house had to look right and both sides had to balance. This led to houses such as Audley End in Essex and Hardwick Hall in Derbyshire. Hardwick Hall was popularly supposed to have 'more glass than wall'. All of these mansions had a great number of private rooms, but the hall was retained as a show-piece — carpeted, richly furnished and tastefully decorated.

Windows were designed to let in more light than formerly, although glass could still only be made in small panes set in lead strips. In the sixteenth century, ceilings began to be plastered, an idea which had originated in Italy. The plaster was moulded into patterns, some of which were very ornate, showing animals, leaves and monograms.

The long gallery on the first floor ran the length of the house and was used

21 (*Top*) The south front of Long-leat House in Wiltshire.

22 (*Above*) An engraving of Hard-wick Hall in Derbyshire.

23 (*Right*) Fountains Hall in York-shire, built with materials from the dissolved Fountains Abbey nearby.

as a place for exercise, conversation and music. It too would be tastefully decorated with strong oak furniture.

Even the gardens surrounding these Tudor mansions were planned down to the last detail. Paths curved in patterns, and flower-beds and hedges were neat and orderly. A parson called William Harrison, writing in 1577, mentioned 300 different plants growing in his own garden.

Timber remained the only building material for the poor, although some wealthy men also used it to build their mansions — as at Okwells near Bray in Berkshire. King Henry VIII, too, built a timber palace, called Nonesuch, in Surrey. But few of these wooden structures have survived into our own times.

In the late sixteenth century, a reaction set in against houses built with jetties. They darkened the already narrow streets in towns. Furthermore, they created problems for the escape of smoke, since floor joists could not be removed to allow smoke to escape through a funnel without weakening the support of the second floor. By the end of the century, jetties were being generally abandoned. Houses no longer had to be built storey by storey; instead, timber walls carried on from the ground to the roof, and the roof was supported by timbers directly from ground level. This meant that the chimney stack could be built inside the house, rather than as an external addition, and it could even be sited in the centre of the building.

The classical buildings of ancient Greece and Rome were studied, as ruins, in Italy and elsewhere in Europe during the sixteenth century, and these styles began to influence builders. They were brought to England as the latest in Italian taste, and were eagerly copied. But copying does not always lead to satisfaction: 'The Englishman Italianate, Is the Devil incarnate' ran the rhyme. Some Elizabethan houses began to look like crude caricatures of Roman designs, with too much ornament and decoration.

Many early Tudor mansions had proved difficult to run, and some of these were altered and renovated in Elizabeth's reign. A number of plans and drawings of houses from the Elizabethan period still exist today. Early in Elizabeth's reign, John Shute published the first textbook on architecture to be printed in English.

Other Buildings

The Gothic style of architecture had been followed after about 1450 by the Perpendicular. Cathedrals and churches became tall, slender and elegant. They began to look like cages of stone — thin frames into which glass was inserted — compared with the bulky heaviness of the past.

Sixteenth-century mansions owed much to the ideas of monastic designs. Hampton Court Palace, approached from the west, has a gatehouse and then a number of quadrangles, similar to the cloisters of an abbey. The same plan is obvious in the colleges of Oxford and Cambridge.

6. The Stuart Age

Sir Edward Coke, Chief Justice of England in the reign of James I (1603-25), believed that 'the house of every one is to him as his castle and fortress, as well as his defence against injury and violence as for his repose'. Even today a householder is reasonably safe in his 'castle', and the police must have a warrant issued by a magistrate before a search can be made of an individual's property.

24 The Long Gallery at Hatfield House. Notice the ornate ceiling and the wall panels.

In his book *The Elements of Architecture* (1624), Sir Henry Wotton described how: 'Well-building hath three conditions, Commodity, Firmness and Delight' — that is, it should be firmly and attractively built. These conditions were mirrored surprisingly sharply in the work of architects and builders in the seventeenth century. Architects travelled abroad and learned from the style of classical architecture, particularly that of Italy. Generally, houses became simpler and plainer on the outside, and were planned from the outset as a single unit. A medieval house had consisted of a group of different buildings. The Tudor house often rambled at many different levels. But a house built in the seventeenth century was a planned entity, with a symmetrical facade. Even the front door was often placed in the centre at the front of the house. Windows were of a similar size and were placed where they would show to advantage the proportions of the whole building. The architect now came to the forefront in the design of houses.

Inigo Jones

One of the greatest architects of the age was Inigo Jones (1573-1652). He had travelled and studied in Italy, and was especially interested in the buildings of the Italian architect Palladio. In 1614, Inigo Jones became Surveyor of the Works to James I. He designed a palace for Charles I, but only managed to build the banqueting hall — which still exists in Whitehall. He also built country houses such as Raynham Hall in Norfolk and Wilton House in Wiltshire. His houses were planned in an orderly fashion, in contrast to the haphazard muddle of the past, when wings had been added on at intervals, and the original effect was lost.

Typical features of an Inigo Jones house include carved and moulded chimney-pieces, ceilings and door-frames, and decorated panels on the staircases. Jones considered the main staircase an important part of the design and gave it a prominent position. The great hall now became much smaller and only a single storey high. Its use had diminished with the advent of many different specific rooms in the house, and progressively the hall became smaller and less elaborate until it reached its modest nineteenth- and twentieth-century proportions. The lord's parlour, sometimes called the salon, now became the most important room in the house.

Mansions

Attention to symmetry and proportion was observed most closely in the building of great houses, which were as much houses for looking at as for living in. They were usually built of stone or of brick and stone, and there was often an attractive flight of steps at the entrance, with pillars sometimes reaching up to the roof. Windows were tall and rectangular. Larger window panes allowed more light inside and could be sited to give a balanced effect from the exterior.

25 (*Above left*) The Spangled Bedroom at Knole House, near Sevenoaks in Kent.

26 (*Above right*) The Ballroom at Knole House, with its extravagant marble chimney-piece, detailed wall frieze and elegant paintings of the past owners of Knole.

Sash windows, that slid up and down to open, began to take the place of casement windows that had opened on hinge-like doors. The glazing bars were made of wood and the glass was fixed in place with putty.

Knole House near Sevenoaks in Kent was built during the reign of James I. It was the ultimate in fashionable design, having 365 rooms — one for every day of the year — guest rooms, bedrooms, dressing-rooms, dining-rooms, withdrawing-rooms and rooms for the host of servants needed to maintain such a vast establishment. Several hundred servants were required to run Knole House, where there are 52 staircases and seven courtyards — one for every week of the year and day of the week respectively.

Gentlemen's Houses

Town houses also had a main entrance doorway with an equal number of sash windows on each side. Mansions needed to look pleasing from all aspects, set as they usually were in open, prominent positions; but town houses often looked elegant only from the front. The unimportant sides and the back were left plain and attention was concentrated on making the front as pleasing and dignified as possible for the price.

The architect grew proficient at achieving a compact, harmonious entity. Early Tudor buildings had been arranged around a courtyard. The Elizabethan architect fitted all rooms required into a block with short side wings attached. But the seventeenth-century designer planned to fit the whole house behind four walls. This created more of a problem than is immediately obvious, for the span of the roof had to be greatly increased as a result. The double-span roof covered a width of two rooms, one at the front and another at the rear of the house. But in case such a roof might appear overpowering, it was largely hidden from view by carrying up the front of the house in the form of a parapet.

John Evelyn, the English diarist, left an interesting account of his travels in

43

the mid-seventeenth century. In 1654 he visited Bath, which was 'entirely built of stone, but the streets narrow, uneven, and unpleasant'. He visited Sir John Glanvill's estate at Broad-Hinton and found the former Speaker of the House of Commons living in his gatehouse, 'his very faire dwelling-house having ben burnt by his owne hands to prevent the rebells making a garrison of it'. These were the troubled times of the Civil War (1642-49), when the country was split in loyalty between Royalists and Parliamentarians.

Evelyn noticed many new houses built in the latest styles, but he was critical of the living conditions he found in most towns, such as 'the old and ragged Citty of Leicester, large and pleasantly seated, but despicably built, the chimney flues like so many smiths' forges'.

Once England was released from the Puritan spirit of plain simplicity with the Restoration of Charles II in 1660, the spirit of ingenuity in furniture was unleashed on chairs and tables, chests and beds, writing desks and stools. Fashionable town-dwellers living in fashionable houses required fashionable furniture to decorate and enhance their homes. The other famous diarist of the time, Samuel Pepys, enjoyed decorating his home as well as he was able. His dining-room had 'greene serge hanging and gilt leather'. Both Pepys and Evelyn were impressed by the decor in the home of a Mr Povey of Lincoln's Inn Fields. Pepys was especially intrigued by the novelty of a bath in Mr Povey's house:

> his room floored above with woods of several colours, like but above the best cabinet-work I ever saw; his grotto and vault with his bottles of wine, and a well therein to keep them cool; his furniture of all sorts; his bath at the top of the house, good pictures, and his manner of eating and drinking; do surpass all that ever I did see of one man in all my life.

In smaller town houses, if the stair rose straight from the entrance in the usual manner, there was a great waste of space, despite the grand effect that such a staircase achieved. The answer to the problem of saving space was the dog-legged stair. This had a small 'half-landing' between the floors, where there was a change in direction. At first stairs of this type were known as 'a pair of stairs'.

A number of squares were planned in London in the seventeenth century, including Leicester Square in 1635 and Bloomsbury Square in 1665. After the Great Fire of 1666, the city grew westwards; Soho Square was built in 1681 and Grosvenor Square in 1695. Solid but elegant houses were planned around these squares, of which St James's (1684) is a foremost example.

Ordinary Homes
Village craftsmen and reasonably well-off farmers in the seventeenth century lived in neat cottages, timber-framed, made of stone or, in the eastern counties,

27 Rubens's ceiling in the Banquet-Hall of the United Services Museum, Whitehall. The panels, completed in 1634, are set in a richly moulded gilded framework. Charles I commissioned Rubens at a fee of £3,000, and then knighted him because of a delay in payment. The canvases have been restored six times.

built of brick. Many farmhouses had two storeys, with a chimney as well as stairs in the centre of the house. Simple cottages usually had one room on each floor with the chimney-stack at one end. But the poor, both in countryside and town, often lived in insanitary hovels. Large town houses and palaces that had been abandoned and were gradually falling to ruin were taken over by squatters who were only too glad to find a roof, even if it leaked. A survey from the early seventeenth century showed that four of these large houses in London were sheltering 8,000 destitute people.

The window tax was introduced in 1697, and survived until 1851. The tax was levied on houses valued at more than £5 a year which had more than six windows. As a result, windows were often bricked over to avoid the tax. Of course, poor people did not have as many as six windows — they might not have glass at all — but if they lived in a room in a larger house then the light and fresh air in the house as a whole might well be lessened.

In 1661, even chimneys became subject to a tax of two shillings (10p) per chimney, but fortunately soon after house-owners were relieved of this tax. It is interesting to speculate what would have happened otherwise, since the design of houses might well have changed to try to dispense with chimneys.

Wealthy landowners in the country, growing rich on the profits from

28 (*Above left*) Arlington Row, Bibury, in Gloucestershire. These seventeenth-century cottages belong to the National Trust.

29 (*Above right*) The royal barge passing Whitehall in the reign of William and Mary, 1690.

overseas trade, also built substantial new cottages for farmworkers with tile or slate roofs and windows covered with glass.

Sir Christopher Wren

In 1661 Christopher Wren was appointed Assistant to the Surveyor General by Charles II. Shortly after, much of London was reduced to ashes in the Great Fire and Wren planned a new city to take its place.

Seventeenth-century London before the fire was still a medieval timbered city, its houses irregularly grouped in insanitary alleys. In his rebuilding, Wren left much of magnificence, and enhanced the London skyline with towers and spires, but his dream of a properly-planned city was not to be. Strong vested interests retained much of the old street system, and little overall planning was achieved. Areas for living in continued to be mixed with industrial sites. John Evelyn even wrote a pamphlet, *Fumifugium*, in which he warned of the dangers of industries producing smoke in the midst of a city, but to no avail.

Wren designed the new St Paul's Cathedral and many other London churches, and houses in the town and countryside. In his work, he was influenced more by French than Italian ideas. He built elegantly and symmetrically, and his Renaissance houses became prototypes for the Georgian houses of the following century.

Many of Wren's churches were built out of Portland stone, and he also used it for some town houses. It was reasonably resistant to acids, and tended to turn from cream to black and white when exposed to rain and smoke. Portland stone was used indeed for the building of much of historic London, but this meant that detailed carving had to be avoided because of the long-term weathering.

The Boom in Bricks

Few areas were as distinctively specialized in regional building materials as were the Cotswolds. There was little suitable timber available locally, so the Cotswold builders became masons, erecting small farmhouses in all parts of the region. In the towns, too, stone was used to build gable-ended houses and some towns were virtually rebuilt in the seventeenth century.

In the country generally, brick was taking over from timber, as timber became a scarce commodity. It was used for many different purposes, as a pamphlet published in 1631 complained:

> timber for Navigation, with infinite increase of building of houses, with the great expense of wood to make household furniture, caskes, and other vessels not to be numbered, and of Carts, Wagons, and Coaches, besides the extreame wast of Wood in making Iron, burning of brick and tile . . .

The denudation of forests as a result of this had worried James I at the start of the seventeenth century. He attacked the building of houses with jetties, and passed acts forbidding buildings in cities that were not faced with stone or brick. Much in these enactments was doubtless flouted, but, in time, no further timber fronts were built in town streets. James could then say: 'We had found our Citie and suburbs of London of stickes, and left them of brick.' Improved though conditions were, however, James's boast was hardly accurate, as the ease with which the Great Fire swept through the city showed only too well.

Brick-works were opened in many parts of the country, usually outside towns. The lower storeys of jettied houses were often rebuilt in brick, and this increased the area of the ground-floor rooms by utilizing the space previously under the jetties.

The size of bricks was controlled by law in 1625: 9 by 4½ by 3 inches (22.9 by 11.4 by 7.6 cm). Previously, bricks had been small, almost like tiles. Now instead of each brick-works deciding on the size of its own bricks, national conformity — or approaching that — made building techniques more standardized and the job of following an architect's instructions became simpler. The rose red of bricks (except in areas where yellow bricks were made) became common in all parts of the country — not only for buildings, but also for high walls around country estates, and even for walled village lanes.

47

7. The Eighteenth Century

Queen Anne Houses

Houses built during the reign of Queen Anne, between 1702 and 1714, share certain common characteristics. The predominant effect was of red brick contrasted with white paint on window frames and doors. The design was neat and simple, and windows and doors were carefully proportioned along classical lines. The sash window went up high, close to the ceiling, to let as much light as possible into the rooms. Most light, in fact, enters a room through the upper part of a window. Often there was a short flight of steps before the front door. The ground floor was therefore sited a little way above the ground, positioned on top of a semi-basement. In time, the basement became a dingy part of the house, and the servants were relegated there.

30 A Queen Anne house at Lyneham in Wiltshire. Notice the first floor windows that have been bricked over — probably to avoid paying window tax.

Georgian Mansions

During the eighteenth century merchants became increasingly wealthy as a result of overseas trade, manufacture and the ownership of land. Many of them invested their wealth in the construction of larger and more comfortable houses. The Georgian mansion was a huge country residence, where entertaining was an integral part of the way of life. There were large numbers of bedrooms and magnificent rooms for entertaining guests, drawing-rooms, dining-rooms, a picture gallery, a music room, a library and a gun-room.

The main building was usually flanked by wings. One wing was for stables and coaches, and the other was the kitchen area. Long passages, with decorative pillars, joined the wings to the main house. The principal rooms were on the first floor, reached from ground level by an impressive staircase. Often the centre of the exterior had a triangular pediment at roof level and was decorated with statues and the coat of arms of the family. The idea of a pediment came from the pediments on ancient Roman temples. A low parapet partly concealed the roof. The roof itself often had domes at the ends and statues.

An army of servants was needed to run such a house — footmen, housemaids, valets, cooks, butlers and scullery-maids — and out of doors gardeners, game-keepers, grooms, stable-boys and coachmen were all kept busy.

Furniture for the rich became graceful and delicate. The grain of the wood was now polished to form the decoration, and the art of veneering — glueing thin sheets of attractively-marked wood over a more ordinary wood — became very popular. Walnut was widely used for veneering. The attractive reddish-brown mahogany was imported from the West Indies from about 1730, but it was not often used for veneers. Thomas Sheraton, George Hepplewhite and Thomas Chippendale were the most popular cabinet-makers of the eighteenth century, and they designed furniture that is still highly-prized and eagerly sought after.

Country mansions were often built by experts from Europe, to the designs of famous architects. Many such mansions survive today: Chatsworth House in Derbyshire was built in the 1680s for the Duke of Devonshire, Woburn Abbey in Bedfordshire was built in the 1740s for the Duke of Bedford, and Blenheim Palace in Oxfordshire was started in 1705 and took 18 years to complete! It was built for the Duke of Marlborough, in part a gift from the nation after his decisive victory over the French at the Battle of Blenheim in 1704, and cost £300,000. It is one of the largest houses in England.

Vanbrugh

Sir John Vanbrugh was the most noted architect of the early eighteenth century. He was made Comptroller of the Royal Works (under Christopher Wren) in 1702. Castle Howard in Yorkshire, Seaton Delaval in Northumberland and Blenheim Palace are amongst his most famous works. He built, as he said,

Eighteenth-century architecture:

31 (*Opposite top*) A substantial eighteenth-century house at Salisbury.

32 (*Opposite*) The dining-room at Hagley Hall, Stourbridge.

33 (*Above*) The south front of Blenheim Palace in Oxfordshire.

34 (*Right*) A corner of one of the rooms at Blenheim, richly furnished and with beautiful oil paintings.

'both for state, beauty and convenience'. The poet Alexander Pope wrote in glowing terms of Blenheim's grandeur — a quality in which Vanbrugh specialized — but was scathing about the use of such a building as a home:

> See, sir, here's the grand approach;
> This way is for his grace's coach:
> There lies the bridge, and here's the clock,
> Observe the lion and the cock,
> The spacious court, the colonnade,
> And mark how wide the hall is made!
> The chimneys are so well design'd,
> They never smoke in any wind.
> This gallery's contrived for walking,
> The windows to retire and talk in;
> The council chamber for debate,
> And all the rest are rooms of state.
> Thanks, sir, cried I, 'tis very fine,
> But where d'ye sleep, or where d'ye dine?
> I find, by all you have been telling,
> That 'tis a house, but not a dwelling.

Another poet, Abel Evans, wrote — as a joke — an epitaph he thought would be suitable for Vanbrugh's grave:

> Under this stone, reader, survey
> Dead Sir John Vanbrugh's house of clay.
> Lie heavy on him, earth! for he
> Laid many heavy loads on thee.

Grounds and Gardens

By the mid-eighteenth century, the owners of many mansions had begun to make use of ruins to enhance the grounds of their estates. Ruined chapels, churches and medieval buildings were regarded as an asset. Some owners even built fake ruins — or 'follies' as they were scornfully called by ordinary country folk. Almost as much thought seems to have gone into planning the site of the mansion as went into the building itself. The grounds surrounding the house were impressive, with an imposing long avenue of trees leading to the main entrance. Landscape gardeners became experts at their craft. Trees were planted so that dark firs and pines would contrast with the lighter colours of oak and elm, and weeping willows became popular. 'Capability' Brown was the most notable landscape gardener of the age. Born Lancelot Brown, he was termed 'Capability' because of his habit of remarking that he saw capabilities —

35 An engraving of the flower garden at Nuneham in Oxfordshire which was laid out by Capability Brown.

or possibilities — of improving a garden. Artificial lakes (as at Blenheim) were created to give magnificent views from the house. No fences were erected, for fear of spoiling such a view; instead a ditch, called a 'ha-ha', was generally dug to stop animals crossing from the meadow to the lawn.

Georgian Town Houses

Georgian town houses were built in blocks and had extensive facades: squares, terraces and crescents were all planned with orderly elegance. Town houses were tall — often four or five storeys — and narrow, perhaps with a street frontage of only one room. Each storey had between two and four rooms. The basement was reached by external steps leading to the servants' day quarters and the kitchens. The front door opened on to a long straight hall, so there had to be a fan-light above the door to let light into the hall. From the hall one staircase led internally down to the kitchens while a larger one led to the upper rooms. The main drawing-room and study were upstairs and further up still were the bedrooms. The servants' bedrooms were on the top floor. The staircases between the floors were long and inconvenient, and numerous servants were needed to run the house efficiently. But such houses were in great demand among businessmen, doctors, lawyers, merchants and even country landowners, who wanted a town house where they could spend part of every year.

Many town houses had a small garden at the rear, where there were also stables and living accommodation for the coachmen. At the front of the house there might be a communal garden on the other side of the road, in the middle of a square. Bath, Edinburgh and London are among the cities that still have fine Georgian squares and crescents. Nowadays, of course, the inconvenience of these high houses makes them especially difficult to maintain without domestic help, and most have been converted into flats or are used as hotels or offices.

Architects in the eighteenth century generally designed an entire street or square. This planning made the street much more dignified than the hotch-potch of medieval buildings that had gone before.

Brick was now common in towns, although stone was still used in areas where local stone was in good supply or where stone was particularly specified. Bath, for instance, was rebuilt in stone early in the eighteenth century. A father and son, both called John Wood, replanned Bath to give the city an orderly tidiness.

One town house, advertised for let in 1710, was probably typical of many:

To be Let, a New, Brick House, Built after the Newest Fashion, the Rooms wainscotted and Painted, Lofty Stories, Marble Foot places to the Chimneys, Sash Windows, glaised with fine Crown Glass, large half Pace Stairs, that 2 People may go up a Breast, in a new pleasant Court planted with Vines, Jesamin, and other Greens, next Door to the Crown near Saracen's Head Inn in Carter Lane, near St Paul's Church Yard, London.

For all the elegant furnishings, wood panelling on walls, moulded and painted ceilings and elaborate candelabra to illuminate the principal rooms, other aspects of life — even in the houses of the wealthy — were still found wanting. Water from pumps and wells was trundled round the streets for sale by carriers, although some newer London houses obtained water direct from the Thames, channelled through small wooden pipes. There were still no baths in houses, few houses had drains, and although sanitation was improved by the emptying of waste by 'night-men' much remained to be done.

36 (*Far left*) One side of the Promenade at Cheltenham in Gloucestershire.

37 (*Left*) Blaise Hamlet, Bristol, is a curiosity in village architecture. John Nash — the architect of Regent Street in London — built nine cottages, each one different.

38 (*Right*) Castle Combe, an attractive stone-built village in Wiltshire. The shelter on the left is a relic from market days of long ago — buyers and sellers could find protection there from the weather.

Ordinary Homes

Cottages continued to be built in much the same way as before, both in villages and in small towns. Some were built as part of a terrace but most were in pairs, the precursors of today's semi-detached. Semi-detached cottages were often single-fronted, but with a room at the back and bedrooms upstairs. The semi allowed more light in than the terrace house, with a window in the side wall giving light to the staircase, without having to arrange a fan-light above the front door. Slightly better houses, for business people, were built in brick, either singly or in terraces. These were small houses in the Georgian style, with long windows, a portico and a parapet to hide the low roof.

Timber-framed houses were also built, but with a difference. This time the walls were covered with boards on the outside, laid horizontally and overlapping the one below. The style was given the name 'weather-boarding' and was introduced from America, where it had been developed as a means of making houses both quickly and cheaply. In some houses bricks were used for the ground floor walls, and weather-boarding for the upper storey.

In Sussex, the upper storey of a small house generally had walls covered with tiles hung on wooden battens. Another idea was to plaster the outside wall and mould the wet plaster into patterns. This produced an attractive finish called pargetting.

Many people, however, still lived in great poverty in miserable hovels. James Boswell toured the north of Scotland with Dr Johnson in 1773, and recorded that some homes were simply huts built over a hole in the ground. The window was plugged with turf at night. Smoke from a peat fire escaped through a hole in the middle of the roof. Such hovels were still to be seen in many parts of Britain at the end of the eighteenth century. The homes of the town artisans had improved slightly, but in the countryside there was very little difference between the homes of an eighteenth-century labourer and a fifteenth-century cottager.

Shops

A shop in a town was an extension of the home from medieval times until the nineteenth century. Even today the owners of some small shops live on the premises, in a flat above or in rooms behind the shop. Georgian shops were built with a central door and a bow window on either side, behind which wares could be attractively displayed. Such shops can still be seen in old streets in many towns.

The Adam Style

Stucco began to be used on town houses at the end of the eighteenth century. At first it was plastered on the brickwork of the ground floor only; it could be painted as a smooth surface and lines could be pressed into it to make an imitation of stone jointing. The four Adam brothers from Scotland brought stucco to England. In Edinburgh they had built in stone as there was an adequate supply, but stucco provided the same effect for their houses in London.

Robert Adam was appointed Architect to the King (George III) in 1762, but he soon gave up the job and devoted his energies to speculative building with his brothers. They bought some property close to the River Thames and built a large block of terraced houses, called the Adelphi, above some arched warehouses. Robert Adam had toured Europe and had studied the ruins of Diocletian's palace in Dalmatia (in Yugoslavia), from which the idea for the Adelphi was derived.

It is worth mentioning here that classical architecture was given an enthusiastic welcome in the eighteenth century. The excavation of the buried cities of Pompeii and Herculaneum aroused great interest and stimulated new ideas, particularly in the interior decoration of houses.

The Adam brothers were fastidious in providing exact classical detail in their buildings. They also planned the fireplaces, decor and furnishings, so that everything harmonized and blended into a perfect whole. Alcoves and pillars were plastered, painted and finished with gilt. Artists were brought from Italy to paint ceilings with patterns and pictures. Elaborate interior decoration was becoming so popular that copy-books of house designs were published to help those not wealthy enough to employ their own architect.

Meanwhile the Frenchman Abbé Laugier and the German Johann Winckleman put forward the idea that Greek architecture was superior to Roman, since Greek building provided a simpler effect. As a result, in time, the style of the Adam brothers was regarded as too elaborate and fussy, as well as too expensive. Nevertheless, Robert Adam achieved tremendous success with such ventures as Syon House in Middlesex, the magnificent mansion which he redesigned for the Duke of Northumberland, and with his imposing town houses in London, such as the Adelphi and Portland Place.

The Regency

The classical styles and elegant interior designs of the Georgian age were continued in the Regency period. This lasted from 1811 to 1830 and was so named because George, Prince of Wales, acted as regent in place of his father, George III, who was steadily going insane. The period saw a continuation of eighteenth-century trends, and so can justifiably fall within the bounds of this chapter.

The Napoleonic Wars with France (1793-1815) tended to slow down the rate of ambitious building projects, and the modest detached villa became typical of Regency times. The Regent was interested in building and was fortunate in having John Nash at his side to turn his ideas into realities. Nash had earlier designed country houses, and when the Regent wanted a plan for Marylebone Park (a large tract of land to the north of London) it was Nash who supplied the details. The Regent was anxious to turn London into a planned city; perhaps he was inspired by the example of Napoleon, who was in the middle of replanning Paris. Marylebone Park, with terraces of houses and a royal pavilion, was renamed Regent's Park. Much of the original plan was never completed, but various terraces that survive (such as Cumberland Terrace built in 1827, and Chester Terrace built in 1825) illustrate the ambitious scheme worked out by Nash. Nash also designed the fantastic Royal Pavilion at Brighton for the Prince Regent.

The Prince Regent became George IV in 1820. In that year Nash began to rebuild Buckingham Palace as a royal residence. Nash was also occupied with various 'Metropolitan Improvements', which culminated in the design of Trafalgar Square in 1830. Another of his famous buildings in London is the Marble Arch, originally built as the principal entrance to Buckingham Palace but re-erected in 1851 on its present site.

Nash faced many buildings with stucco, not just on the lower storeys as Robert Adam had done, but all over the brickwork. Stucco is now usually painted white or cream, but Nash intended it to resemble Bath stone when painted. He was criticised at the time for his wholesale use of stucco instead of the traditional brick finish:

> Augustus at Rome was for building renown'd,
> And of marble he left what of brick he had found;
> But is not our Nash, too, a very great master?
> He finds us all brick and he leaves us all plaster.

Sir John Soane was a contemporary of Nash. He also worked in London, replanning for example the Bank of England, and building Dulwich College Picture Gallery. He was an austere architect and believed that the façade of a building needed essentials only.

The centres of large towns were brightened in this period by the addition of various public buildings, including town halls; many churches were also built. The 'Million Pound Act' of 1818 enabled 214 churches to be erected in the growing industrial towns.

39 (*Left*) Chester Terrace, built by John Nash near Regent's Park.

40 (*Below left*) The dining room at the Royal Pavilion in Brighton.

41 (*Below right*) The Strand, London, in the early nineteenth century.

42 (*Opposite*) Dog Leap Stairs, Newcastle-upon-Tyne, about 1880.

8. Victorian Buildings

Population Increase

Two revolutions, more than any others, have vitally affected the development of mankind: the agricultural and the industrial revolutions. The Agricultural Revolution can be said to have begun in Britain with the arrival of primitive farmers in the second millennium BC. This revolution transformed hunters and food-gatherers into farmers and shepherds. The Industrial Revolution in turn transformed these farmers and shepherds into operators of machinery, which was fed with inanimate energy. The Industrial Revolution in Britain was the product of economic, social and cultural changes that had taken place between the mid-sixteenth and the eighteenth and early nineteenth centuries.

Power, mainly water power, had been used to drive looms in the cotton industry in the eighteenth century. In 1750 there had been about 40,000 hands employed by the industry; however, by 1830, this figure had risen to 800,000. Great ironworks were opened near coalfields because the new blast furnaces needed coal and coke. Steam power began to be used to drive machinery. The cotton and woollen mills and iron foundries grew into vast concerns; and the railways arrived to carry the coal, to make the steam, to all parts of the country.

The Industrial Revolution created a large urban population, who were massed together in poverty and misery in the factory towns. After Britain's transformation into an industrial nation, between 1801 and 1914, the country's population quadrupled.

The first official census of the population of England and Wales took place in 1801. However it is still possible to estimate, if somewhat imperfectly, the population before that time. England and Wales probably had a population of about 1½ million on the eve of the Norman Conquest (1066). This increased in some ages and decreased in others, as in the fourteenth century when the infamous Black Death killed off about a third of the population. But gradually the excess of births over deaths rose, so that by 1700 the population of England and Wales was about six million. By the time of the first census in 1801, this had increased to 8.9 million — a rise of about 2.9 million during the eighteenth century. Then, in the nineteenth century, population rocketed. By 1901 it had increased to 32.5 million, a rise of 23.6 million in a single century. The change was due less to a rise in the birth rate than to a fall in the death rate, a fall which can be largely attributed to better food, immunity and resistance to disease and gradual medical reform.

Even so, the evils of overcrowding in towns became very great. In 1840, there were 15,000 people in Manchester living in cellars. One Liverpool physician described the back-to-back houses as being 'in the most abominable state of filth'. Rows of houses were usually built about three to five metres apart, but in one case they were a mere two metres apart. The factory towns began to swarm with people who were only too eager to take a room, an attic

43 A poor working man's home – a single room.

or the corner of a cellar in which to house themselves and their luckless dependents.

In 1773, Manchester had been a small town of about 14,000 people. By 1788 it had a population of 50,000. In three years, by 1791, this grew to 70,000, and by 1801 to 75,000. Other new towns, as well as some old ones, also grew very quickly – giving rise to social and health problems to which there seemed no ready answer. The dangerous consequences of overcrowding in towns were not understood until it was much too late.

Friedrich Engels's book, *The Condition of the Working Class in England in 1844*, contains much accurate social research. He described how artisans and their families lived in insanitary slums: 'the streets are generally unpaved, rough, dirty, filled with vegetable and animal refuse, without sewers or gutters, but supplied with foul stagnant pools instead'.

In St Giles, a working-class area near Trafalgar Square, the houses were crowded from attic to cellar. Few panes of glass remained in the windows, walls were crumbling and doors were loose or made of old boards: 'Heaps of garbage and ashes lie in all directions and the foul liquids emptied before the doors gather in stinking pools'. It was not unusual to find a husband and wife, several children and even grandparents living, eating and sleeping in one room. Engels quoted from *The Times*: 'within the most courtly precincts of the richest society of God's earth there may be found night after night, winter after winter, women – young in years – old in sin and suffering – outcasts from society – rotting from famine, filth and disease'.

Houses were built cheaply, and as many as possible were squeezed into the space available. The outside appearance of the house was given almost no thought. Most were plain and shoddy from the outset, and the interiors simple. Many had no running water and no sanitation. A communal tap and communal privies – where waste rapidly accumulated – were sometimes provided.

Older cities also saw a large increase in population. There was no control over the way housebuilders worked – they could not be compelled to drain or sewer the ground – and some new streets in York, for example, as late as

the mid-nineteenth century, were undrained and unpaved, full of holes and ruts and deep in mud. The builder, having bought his land, could put up as many houses as he was able and usually gave not a second thought to drainage, sanitation or the health of those who were to live in them.

There were no cellar dwellings in York, except the basement kitchens of the newer houses, but the poorer classes did not live in these. Instead, the poor occupied the large houses and their outbuildings, which had once been the mansions of the wealthy and were now sub-let as 'apartments'. Very few had sewers. In one area called Bedern — once a fashionable quarter of buildings occupied by ecclesiastics attached to York Minster — there were 98 families in the 1840s living crammed together. 67 families had only one room to be used for all purposes, 18 families had two rooms and only 13 had three rooms or more. One entire building was sub-let in single rooms to 16 families. The staircase windows were made so that they could not open, and the rooms were low so that light was almost totally excluded. The walls and ground were damp. Two filthy privies provided sanitation for the entire house. Against the back wall of some houses dunghills were piled; the fluid from them soaked into the house bringing with it disgusting smells and the very real threat of disease.

Four-roomed cottages were soon occupied by three or four families. Party walls separating the houses were sometimes only a single brick thick, and sound not only travelled from room to room but from house to house. By 1850 overcrowding was acute. In London four families were found living in one room — each family inhabiting a corner.

John Nash the architect complained of shoddy, speculative building:

the sale of the house . . . is the ultimate object of the builders and to this . . . everything out of sight is sacrificed . . . that no defects in the constructive and substantial parts make their appearance while the houses are on sale; and it is to be feared that . . . a very few years will exhibit crooked walls, swagged doorways, bulging fronts, crooked roofs, leaky gutters, inadequate drains and other ills of an originally bad constitution.

Slum Tenements

In the parish of St Denis in York, as many as 11 people were found to be sleeping in the same room; and just over a quarter of the families seen by the district visitors lived in one room only. Of 1,418 dwellings, 460 were described as damp and cold. The poverty-stricken families did not remain long at any one address. In the poorest areas of York, it was found that 27 per cent had lived there for less than a year. Frequent removal seems to have been caused by unhealthy and uncomfortable conditions, as well as the search for work. Richard Thomas, a surgeon in York, remarked:

> There are many houses which are totally unfit for human habitations; they are occupied by the poor Irish, and they are not fit even for pig-sties . . . They get the money upon which they live as well as they can. They beg, or they commence the trade of chopping wood, and send their children with it into the streets to sell. They are nearly naked, and, of course, when anything happens then the parish is the only refuge. They are always at the relieving officer's door, and, of course, a great deal of money is spent.

Engels found appalling conditions in Scotland, in Edinburgh, as well as in England: 'all refuse, garbage and excrements of at least 50,000 persons are thrown into the gutters every night . . . water can be had only from the public pumps and the difficulty of obtaining it naturally fosters all possible filth.'

Building blocks of flats proved to be a useful way of housing large numbers when space was restricted. Blocks of these tenements appeared in many towns — especially in Scotland. Ideally, each family lived in its own flat. Many tenements were three or four storeys high, with several flats at each level.

Other houses were built back-to-back — that is they were joined to the back of houses in the next street. These houses saved space and could be built cheaply, but doors and windows could only be put on outside walls — at the front and perhaps at the side at the end of a terrace — so there was no ventilation through the whole house. Yet miserable though these houses appear by twentieth-century standards, they seemed comfortable enough to the displaced peasants and Irish migrants, many of whom had been used to still inferior dwellings before coming to England. It was not so much the housing that was at fault, as the massing of people in insanitary conditions where germs and disease flourished only too easily.

Water Supply

Water for drinking was supplied in pipes by private companies, but only to the more prosperous parts of towns. The poor were lucky if there was a communal standpipe in the yard, turned on for a limited period each day sometimes for as little as 10 or 15 minutes. Water carriers also toured the streets, with carts

45 Bricklayers at work, about 1895. Their work was often shoddy, so that many houses were defective from the start.

selling water (usually infected) by the pail.

Water was pumped unfiltered from a river, although filters were sometimes used privately by middle- and upper-class families. Sewage drains, if they existed at all, were discharged into the same river, although at a point further downstream from the source of supply. The effect of this on other towns down the river was not considered important. River water 'is usually so turbid and dirty as scarcely to be fit for washing, and still less for cooking, or for being drunk'. Wells were another source of water, but this was not very pure either. Sometimes wells were tainted by the drainage from burial grounds or even from nearby leaking cesspits.

Charles Kingsley, author of *The Water Babies*, was horrified when in the mid-nineteenth century he visited Bermondsey in London, where cholera was rife: 'Oh God! What I saw! People having no water to drink — hundreds of them — but the water of the common sewer which stagnated full of dead fish, cats and dogs under their windows.'

Sanitation

In 1844, 53 overflowing cesspits were discovered under Windsor Castle, accounting for the ailments suffered by the Castle staff. Also in the 1840s, a scientist prepared a report on the state of the drains under Buckingham Palace, but he found conditions so shocking that the report was put quietly to one side. The nineteenth-century trend towards clean and sanitary living seems to have owed little to the example of the wealthy. At Queen Victoria's accession, in 1837, there was no bath at Buckingham Palace; and a London firm openly displayed this advertisement:

Tiffin and Son
Bug-destroyers to Her Majesty.

Evidence of the defective state of town life was collected by several public enquiries in the early 1840s, and some especially important work was done by the Royal Commission on the State of Large Towns. Its first report was issued in 1844. Of 50 towns studied, scarcely a single one had satisfactory drainage, and in 42 the drainage was definitely bad. In 1844, Dr Southwood-Smith formed the Health of Towns Association, whose propaganda forced Parliament to accept Lord Morpeth's Public Health Act of 1848 which created a General Board of Health.

It was indeed time for the government to take the lead in the fight for reform in the towns. A statement made by Canon Harcourt of York, in 1831, still held good for many towns in the middle of the century:

> The want of sufficient common sewers, and the general imperfection of the whole drainage of the city is placed in the strongest light by the reports of the District Boards . . . The slaughter-houses, dung-heaps, pig-sties etc which unfortunately subsist in the heart of the town, are represented in several instances as pouring their fetid contents into open drains, and the effluvia to be sometimes such as might alone suffice to generate contagion.

The houses in the lower parts of streets close to a river were often flooded. Afterwards the floors remained damp for months, yet families had to continue to live there. Worse still was the inefficient disposal of sewage. Houses for the well-off sometimes had water closets emptying into drains and cesspits, but in most cases sanitation was provided by privies. Newer cottages might have one privy per house, but commonly a single privy was shared by up to 14 families. The soil-holes were usually open and were always running over, flooding the back courts. During wet weather privies were often emptied by bucket into an open channel in the middle of the street. People living in houses without privies had to sneak into neighbours' privies or use the street. When a sufficient quantity had accumulated privies were emptied by night and the refuse carted away in barrows to large dung-hills within the city, where it was sold to manure merchants.

Dirt and Disease

Coal was the usual fuel for heating; gas-light was used extensively, both in the home and at work. There was no escape from the bad air which they produced. Factories poured smoke into the atmosphere, polluting bodies and damaging furniture and clothing. In York, a relatively small city, the following factories and businesses each produced smoke:

Steam-engines	28
Glass-works	2
Iron-foundries	3
Coach-manufacturers	6
Pipe-manufacturers	3

Bakers	25
Confectioners	7
Brewers	14
Smiths	35
Total	123

Fresh air was usually lacking in most towns. A chemist, W White, published a pamphlet in 1845 in which he discussed the importance of fresh air, water and the circumstances affecting sanitary conditions. The effect of an atmosphere charged with evil-smelling gases had long been known, and bye-laws prohibited the erection of pig-sties and similar nuisances within certain boundaries; but these regulations were generally obsolete and were ignored except when an epidemic caused alarm. White suggested two methods for securing an adequate supply of fresh air. The first was to allow for the free circulation of air in dwellings and other buildings. He believed that the clergy and district visitors could help by pointing out to the poor the need to renew air in their homes by adequate ventilation. Secondly, the means and opportunity for frequent exercise in the open air were necessary. Parks and other spaces should be provided in every town for the convenience of the inhabitants.

Cholera originated in India; the first case diagnosed in Britain was at Sunderland in October 1831. It was a disease of dirt, poor sanitation and infected drinking water. The victim suffered violent stomach pains and vomiting, and usually died within a short space of time. There were major outbreaks in British towns in the 1830s, '40s, '50s and '60s. Typhus also struck in the poorer parts of London in 1838, claiming many victims.

Improving Conditions

Lord Normanby, Home Secretary, realized the need for government leadership. But his Bill of 1839 to regulate building methods was strongly opposed in many quarters, an indication of the strength of those interested in preserving the existing insanitary dwellings. But slowly conditions improved. Henry Doulton opened a factory at Lambeth in 1846 to make glazed stoneware pipes. These made possible efficient drainage. Edwin Chadwick fought long and earnestly for decent living standards in towns, and his efforts achieved some measure of success. Between 1848 and 1853, 284 towns applied for the Board of Health's aid — in search of health and happiness for several million souls.

The Public Health Act of 1875 covered water supplies, the drainage of undrained houses, the collection of household refuse, street cleaning and sewage disposal. Although London's death rate did not fall substantially until the 1870s, the drop came soon after the new drainage system was opened. This consisted of about 83 miles of intercepting sewers, carrying 420 million gallons daily.

George Smith's pamphlet, *The Bitter Cry of Outcast London* (1883), dwelt on the appalling state of the city's dwellings. The Royal Commission on Housing sat during 1884-85 — even the Prince of Wales was a member — and concluded that the speculative builder was still exclusively concerned with profit and gave little thought to comfort and convenience in the houses he was building.

Even so, progress did come, if only slowly. Local authorities began to insist that houses must have a minimum number of rooms, that walls were to be of a minimum thickness and that every house must have a sink in the kitchen and also a lavatory with proper facilities for sewage disposal. But there is no date in history at which we can claim that the evils of town life ended. Even today, people live in slum properties, and town councils are still making great efforts to obliterate them and rehouse the inhabitants in modern, well-built houses and flats. Think carefully about these figures:

In one area lived 3,200 families.
The area contained only 280 baths.
Only 65 families had their own separate lavatory.
388 families were without a separate piped water supply.
Only 153 families out of 3,200 had all 'mod-cons', that is, hot and cold water, bath and lavatory.

This was not a survey made in a town in the nineteenth century. No. It was made in part of typhoid-struck Aberdeen in the early 1960s, in an area which exhibited a blue-print design for an epidemic. Such figures remind us forcibly that there can never be room for relaxation or complacency in the fight for a minimum standard of living for all.

Model Dwellings

Various experiments were carried out in the attempt to erect working-class dwellings and flats of a high standard. On Merseyside in the 1840s, for example, four-storey buildings were erected in red brick, with two homes on each floor. Each block of buildings had a communal staircase and each flat had a living-room, two bedrooms, scullery and lavatory. The living-room was fitted with gas for lighting, and the flats were ventilated with cold air. One critic of these flats for dock labourers complained that the buildings did not provide warm air ventilation!

Model houses were erected at the Cavalry Barracks in Hyde Park in 1851 by Prince Albert. These consisted of four flats: two up and two down. The houses were supplied with fresh air, sunlight and drainage. Each house had a living-room, three bedrooms, a scullery, lavatory and lobby. In the scullery was a sink with a coal box below it, a plate rack, a meat safe and a rubbish shaft for refuse disposal. The living-room had a cupboard on one wall, warmed by the fireplace, and there was also a linen cupboard. Windows were large and uncluttered. The design could be built up to four storeys high.

Many charitable trusts were set up in the late nineteenth century, as an expression of the 'social conscience' of the time. One notable example was the Peabody Trust established by George Peabody, a rich American who lived in London. Peabody spent a fortune in building houses for the poor. By 1875 nearly 4,000 people were living in blocks of tenements he had erected, the first of which, built of brick and mortar, was opened in 1864. They may have looked dreary, but at least each family had a home of its own — sharing was forbidden.

Municipal flats were built from the 1860s onwards — the first step in acknowledging the duty of municipalities to provide housing for the poor or homeless. Gradually it became accepted that planning a town was primarily the concern of those who applied and enforced public health laws and regulations. As a result, it was the Ministry of Health which was given responsibility for housing. The idea of creativity and attractive design in housing in town centres was for the time being lost.

The Battle of the Styles

The overcrowded town centres encouraged people to build in new areas around a town. The suburbs on the outskirts were usually inhabited by the well-off, who were glad to pay for space, trees and fresh air. Suburban housing often imitated the Gothic styles of medieval times with pointed roofs, pointed windows and perhaps a porch. Some Victorian Gothic houses look most peculiar — with their towers, ornate battlements and decorative brickwork. The wealthy wanted their prosperity to be recognized, and a grand-looking house was considered essential. The middle-class home had become, in modern jargon, a status

symbol. Even inside the house everything was ornate and colourful. There was little space to spare in the parlour, with its excess of furniture and ornamentation. Cuthbert Bede's *Adventures of Mr Verdant Green* describes the rooms of a wealthy Oxford undergraduate:

> There were round tables and square tables, and writing tables, and there were side tables with statuettes and Swiss carvings, and old china, and gold apostle-spoons, and lava ware, and Etruscan vases, and a swarm of elegant knick-knackeries.

Houses and their interiors were 'put into fancy dress' and good design no longer meant good proportion. The well-known critic and reformer John Ruskin encouraged Gothic tastes:

> Do not think of unities of effect. Introduce your Gothic line by line and stone by stone; never mind mixing it with your present architecture; your existing houses will be none the worse for having little bits of better work fitted to them; build a porch, or point a window, if you can do nothing else; and remember that it is the glory of Gothic architecture that it can do *anything*.

That many agreed with Ruskin is shown by the number of Victorian Gothic buildings that still exist today. The rise of such individualism in building resulted in very haphazard street planning — each house was designed without any thought for the others in the road.

The battle of the styles — classical versus Gothic — continued through the nineteenth century, although Gothic had largely won the battle by the start of Victoria's reign in 1837. Yet imitation of past designs is seldom successful in

46 (*Far left*) Peabody Square Model Dwellings, Blackfriars Road, London.

47 (*Left*) A Victorian drawing-room filled with ornaments — a nightmare for the housemaid who had to dust and clean.

48 (*Right*) A mid-Victorian mansion at Barningham in Yorkshire. Notice the double attics and the Tudor-style chimneys.

architecture, and a great many Victorian buildings today stand out as tasteless mixtures. Robert Kerr, in *The Gentleman's House* (1864), lists the qualities which were regarded as necessary for good housing in the 1860s: 'Privacy, Convenience, Spaciousness, Compactness, Light and Air, Salubrity, Aspect, Prospect, Cheerfulness, Elegance, Importance and Ornament'.

Charles Voysey (1857-1941) was a well-known architect who followed only his own style. He built country houses to a very simple design, using stone, slate roofs and large chimney-stacks. Low eaves gave his buildings a horizontal, spacious feeling. Internal woodwork he usually painted white, to provide an atmosphere of lightness and freshness.

Another famous architect, Sir Edwin Lutyens (1869-1944) built both terrace cottages and large country houses in the 1890s. Lutyens was interested in classical styles, and although his work had no long-term effect, his influence may have retarded the modern movement in styles by providing his own brand as an alternative. Indeed, it was clear that the love of the classical style was not yet dead when, in 1862, Lord Palmerston refused a Gothic design for the Foreign Office in Whitehall — an enclave of classical building.

The Great Exhibition

Sir Joseph Paxton's Crystal Palace was built in 1851 of iron, glass and wood, in prefabricated units that were assembled on the site. It was the setting for the Great Exhibition of that year and the building itself — a great glass cage — looked forward to the age of iron. Iron soon became common in the construction of churches and other such buildings. The Crystal Palace housed a display of the worst and the best machine-made industrialized products which were to dominate life and fill the corners of every room for the remainder of the nineteenth century.

Improvement in Services

Tap water gradually became common, as did outside lavatories — bathrooms were still rare in houses built for the working class.

Electric lighting was introduced into towns from about 1890. Many people found the new form of lighting a novelty, as the following tale relates:

In 1889 we stayed at an hotel in Southampton that had electricity installed and our mother, who wasn't sure how to switch it on, had to ring for the maid to ask her how to do it. In 1890 we were living in what was then a small town in Yorkshire and ours was the first home in the town to be lighted with electricity. We generated our own power. People living in the town used to drive up to our gates in carriages, and also bring their visitors, to see the house with the lights. As young children, when we heard the sound of horses' hooves at dusk in our quiet road we rushed round the house

49 (*Above left*) The Crystal Palace Exhibition of 1851.

50 (*Above right*) Cober Hill, Cloughton, in Yorkshire, built in 1890. The fussy architectural detail of earlier Victorian decades has been avoided here.

51 (*Left*) St Pancras Station in London.

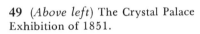

switching the lights on and off so that the spectators outside would not be disappointed.

The same person remembers the installation of an early telephone:

We also had a telephone installed in 1890. This consisted of a large walnut box fixed on the wall and which sloped at the top with a ledge for the telephone book. There was a handle which had to be turned and a bar on the telephone that had to be pressed tightly or the connection would be lost. Telephones were then very much a novelty and there was no acknowledged position in the home in which to install them. Ours was installed in the bathroom as this was a place where a call could be made quietly and in private. Later we went to the other extreme and had the telephone moved into the hall. Once, some visitors to our home, after inspecting the telephone, refused to believe that it actually worked. So mother rang a fruiterer to order some fruit and vegetables and it was only when the order arrived that the visitors were convinced!

Railway Stations and Opera Houses

A large number of public buildings were constructed in the second half of the nineteenth century. Some, such as railway stations, served completely new needs. More traditionally, libraries, law courts, town halls and museums sprang up everywhere as well as offices of many different kinds.

The Houses of Parliament had been destroyed by a fire in 1834 and were rebuilt between 1840 and 1860 by Sir Charles Barry, aided by A W N Pugin. The Gothic design, with its perpendicular emphasis, was a fitting style for a building whose roots were steeped in history.

Between 1849 and 1859 William Butterfield built All Saints, in Margaret Street, London, using a Gothic style with colour as the keynote. Then, in the 1860s, came a building boom in hotels — following the advent of railways to take people to the seaside. Some of them, such as the Grand Hotel at Scarborough (built 1863-67) show a French influence — as do Grosvenor Gardens, Hyde Park Corner and Redcliffe Square in London — with oval windows, projecting porches and short Corinthian columns.

Euston, St Pancras and King's Cross were three of the most interesting railway stations built in London at this time. Euston Station was demolished in 1965, but it used to be classical in style, with large pillars; King's Cross has two huge curved roofs over the platforms, with a clock-tower; and St Pancras has a fairy-tale, romantic appeal.

Music-halls and public houses abounded in every town. Few music-halls are now left standing, but Victorian theatres still remain — such as the Royal Opera House, Covent Garden (1856), which was designed by E M Barry.

9. Twentieth-Century Architecture

Semi-Detached Comfort

Homes have improved steadily since the start of the twentieth century. Before 1900 bathrooms were rare, but soon after began to be fitted as a matter of course, following the installation of a hot water system that was heated from a boiler, often sited behind the fire in the living-room. Later, gas and electric heaters allowed for hot baths without using the open fire. Electricity became a standard requirement, and power points in each room prepared the way for the electric revolution and such varying refinements as table lamps, vacuum

52 Many people now live on suburban housing estates. The size of gardens, as this aerial view shows, often depends on the luck of a particular site.

cleaners, radios and refrigerators.

Most buildings followed the semi-detached pattern. These were cheaper to build than detached houses, but gave a feeling of privacy and space often lacking in a terraced house. Many of these houses had a fair-sized garden at the rear and a small one at the front. Most were built of brick with slate roofs, although some walls were coated with plaster and sometimes thousands of tiny stones — known as rough-cast — were embedded while the plaster was still wet. Each house had a small entrance hall, a main living-room (and perhaps a second one), two or three bedrooms, a kitchen, a bathroom and a lavatory. Most builders adopted the 'universal' plan of siting at least one ground floor room at the front and another at the back of the house, so ensuring that some sunshine entered the house during the day.

After the First World War (1914-18), the government allowed local councils to erect houses and rent them to tenants. Before that, most buildings had been financed by private enterprise, but the postwar need for many new houses led to government action. Houses appeared most often by the sides of the main roads leading out of town, which had recently been constructed to carry the motor car. Ribbon development, as it is called, gouged its way into the countryside and created a new being — the commuter — who lived in the suburb and travelled to work in the town. Some speculative builders used shoddy materials and these 'jerry-builders', as they were known, sold houses of poor quality to the gullible buyer.

The bungalow — a single storey house originating in India as a *bangla* — became popular. Elderly people liked the convenience of not having to climb stairs. It was often cheap to build a bungalow because foundations and walls supported only the roof — not an upper storey — and shorter runs of pipework reduced plumbing costs. There is now a tremendous variety in size and type, including those with several rooms in the roof space. A bungalow can be made to look as attractive and imposing as any modern house, and many people today, not only the elderly, prefer a bungalow to a two-storey house.

Garden Cities

In 1902, Ebenezer Howard published *Garden Cities of Tomorrow,* in which he suggested that a small town of about 32,000 people was the best size for a community. At the centre should be schools, shops, public buildings and churches, and the town should be surrounded by countryside that was easily accessible. Industry and other forms of employment should be close at hand, not completely separated from the living areas. Letchworth, built in 1903, was the first 'garden city', followed by Welwyn in 1920. Houses were built in groups in closes, crescents and small side-roads to avoid long rows of buildings.

The garden suburb idea was not quite new, for various private ventures in the nineteenth century — the Cadbury suburb of Bournville (1879) for instance —

53 (*Above left*) Modern town planning at Plymouth. Buses bring passengers close to the shopping precinct, and there are tree-lined walks and places to sit in the sun.

54 (*Above right*) Part of the new Coventry Cathedral, which is linked to the ruins of the old bombed cathedral on the left.

had aimed at housing the workers of a particular firm in such surroundings. But now the garden city was made a public concern, open to anyone. The idea was copied, with varying degrees of success, in all parts of the country and builders began to call any area with a few trees in it a garden suburb. Gardens became larger, and the cramped narrow streets of the old towns began to lose appeal for many people. The influence of the garden suburb is still exerted today in just about every suburban housing development, with its insistence on variety, openness and spacious living.

Housing Estates

Building programmes were cut or abandoned during the First World War, resulting in an acute shortage of housing when hostilities ended in 1918. Architects were quickly commissioned by local authorities to plan new housing estates and many of these were influenced by the garden suburb ideal. Families were rehoused from slum property in the town centre and young families were also anxious to obtain a modern council house at reasonable rent.

An even greater wave of building was necessary at the end of the Second World War in 1945. In the London borough of West Ham more than 14,000

75

houses, out of a total of 50,800, had to be demolished and rebuilt as a result of enemy bombing. Many other cities — such as Plymouth and Coventry — also suffered badly, and their centres have had to be completely rebuilt.

System Building

In 1945 Britain was short of one million homes, and building materials were expensive and difficult to obtain. The prefabricated house was the temporary answer to this. The 'prefab' was made in sections at a factory and then assembled on site. One group of skilled men could erect dozens of prefabs every day. They were small and built close together, because they were only intended to be temporary. Walls were made of weather-resisting board or aluminium sheeting that was warm in winter and cool in summer. The roof, almost flat, was tar-spread. Each prefab contained a sitting-room, one or two bedrooms, a kitchen and a bathroom. All the 150,000 that were built were supposed to last between five and ten years at the most, but some are still being used today and there are even council waiting lists to obtain one. Inevitably, the days of the remaining prefabs must be numbered because, structurally, they will not last much longer — but other forms of prefabricated buildings are only just appearing.

Bricks are heavy to handle. An ordinary, single-car garage has about 2,000 bricks and weighs five tonnes. These bricks may have to be moved by hand as many as six times on their journey from the brick kilns to the walls, for instance, of the garage. Some builders are now experimenting with building methods that do not involve this constant moving of heavy materials, by measuring and making parts of a building off the site. Doors, windows and plumbing fittings have been standardized for many years. They are made by a few firms and supplied to building sites all over the country. Yet there is perhaps even now an unnecessarily large number of different shapes and sizes, and further standardization would reduce costs still more.

In prefabricated buildings a great deal of the work is carried out in the factory. Some firms supply factory-made houses, classrooms, offices, factories and other buildings. The floor, roof and wall panels are fixed in position by a crane. Then the doors and windows are added on. The Timber Research and Development Association (TRADA) have developed similar systems for timber-framed houses.

Prefabrication results in the quick erection of new buildings, and work does not stop because of bad weather. The system reduces excessive labour costs. But to effect substantial economies factory-made buildings, especially houses, need to be ordered in large numbers (for instance, by local authorities) so that the full effects and savings of mass-production can be felt. The mass-produced units are fixed together by a small group of men using power-tools. Once the foundations have been laid, such a building rises by the hour. In fact, the finishing off and installation of services take longer than the erection of the building itself.

Blocks of Flats

A great many modern buildings have a framework of steel or reinforced concrete. The spaces that are left are then filled in, but these 'walls' do not support the building. The walls — whether of plate glass, aluminium or concrete — are just a skin to clothe the structure. Some houses have been made by this method, but normally it is used to construct factories and flats. Buildings can be made as high as required. Flats have electric lifts and some have recreation areas and dining-rooms. But high-rise flats (from 8 to 15 or more storeys) create problems: what to do with young children who want to play outside, people afraid of heights, noise and loneliness. High-rise housing is usually found in large cities where there are problems of finding land on which to build. Medium-rise flats (up to about 8 storeys) are now more usual, and some towns also have low-rise flats of only two or three storeys. Flats often have such facilities as central heating, a central supply of hot water and rubbish disposal shutes. The flat roof can be used to dry clothes and there is space on the ground floor to store push-chairs and bicycles. Some flats also have a garage block.

In Britain, it is more expensive to build blocks of flats than it is to erect semi-detached houses. In fact, building costs for flats are sometimes double those for a two-storey house. Paradoxically, in parts of Sweden, for instance, it is cheaper to build flats than two-storey houses. Climate provides much of the explanation. In a cold country a house with four external walls is difficult to insulate and expensive to heat. In Britain many people make do with inadequate house insulation for the relative spaciousness, privacy and garden which a semi-detached offers.

55 The Memorial Theatre at Stratford.

56 This motor hotel on the outskirts of Leicester is conveniently situated for the M.1. There are large parking spaces for cars. Rooms have a private bath, television and radio; and meals are taken as 'extras'.

Functional Building

Even a cursory glance at a block of flats is usually enough to give an impression either of modern, streamlined attractiveness or of a rather dismal, uninteresting building. But inside, the rooms, facilities and services are as modern — sometimes more so — than those found in two-storey semis. So which is more important: appearance or utility? There is much disagreement on this question. Some argue one way, some another, and others still are convinced that beauty and usefulness *can* go together.

In the late 1930s the French architect Le Corbusier coined the phrase 'The house is a machine for living in'. He believed that an architect should be intelligent, cool and calm in building a house and laying out a town. Le Corbusier thought that just as motor-car bodies were stamped out in thousands, house frameworks could be made in the same way. Such parts included reinforced concrete. He even dreamed of mass-produced cities, and enormous skyscrapers each housing thousands of families (not hundreds as at present). Le Corbusier built a colony in the south of France that has been studied by architects from all parts of the world — studied but not imitated. The generation of progressive architects who hung on Le Corbusier's words tended to forget that decoration, privacy and comfort have always been necessary features of the Englishman's 'castle'. Yet there is much in Le Corbusier's work that has had lasting effect. He designed flat-roofed concrete houses for the wealthy and thought that a house was incomplete without built-in furniture — cupboards and tables in kitchens and wardrobes in bedrooms were essential.

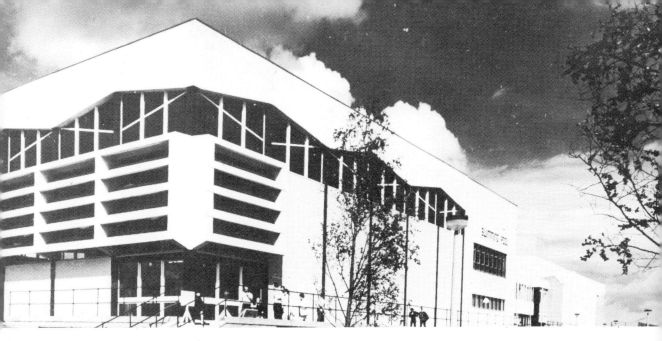

57 A swimming pool and sports centre at Glenrothes New Town, Fife, Scotland.

To use the available internal space to full advantage, halls were dispensed with in some modern houses and the ground floor became one large living area. The sitting-room, dining-room and even the kitchen sometimes form a single large space, and the staircase may even lead directly up from this room. Such open-plan designs have few dividing walls and so create a feeling of spaciousness. One drawback is the lack of privacy; a bedroom large enough to take a comfortable chair becomes important for each member of the family. Open-planning is not only found in houses, but also in schools and offices.

Insulation
British homes, traditionally, have been badly heated. Beside a fire in the sitting-room was usually the only place in winter where the family could get warm. Wealthier people, of course, had bedroom fires, but for most people, before the days of electric fires and rubber hot water bottles, bedrooms were cold.

Nowadays, flats, blocks of offices, shops and an increasing number of individual houses are centrally heated. This is often achieved by hot water pipes which run under the floorboards and are connected to radiators in each room, with the power coming from a central boiler. The water is heated by oil, gas or solid fuel, and is pumped round the system. Electric storage heaters contain bricks that retain heat. Some houses have heat coming through small grills in the ceiling or the floor. A house with central heating allows the occupants to keep warm whichever room they go into.

With the world fuel shortage growing worse, it is becoming increasingly costly to heat buildings, especially since much of the heat is lost almost immediately. Heat penetrates through floors, walls, windows, ceilings and the fireplace, but much can be done to reduce heat-loss by effective insulation of the house. The fireplace can be blocked with a piece of peg-board, with small holes in it to allow some ventilation. Fitted carpets help to reduce heat-loss through the floor, and rolls of fibre-glass can be laid in the loft — the more layers the better. Secondary windows or double-glazed sealed units reduce wastage of heat through windows, and the cavity wall can be filled from the outside with expanded plastic foam.

The New Towns
Since the last war and the New Towns Act of 1946 new towns have been developed. These are large complex communities which need careful planning. Fifteen new towns had been established by 1960, and others have since followed. Each town is divided into 'neighbourhoods' housing about 5,000 people with a central meeting-hall which can be used for all different activities. Such new towns include Harlow, Bracknell, Stevenage, Crawley, Corby, Peterlee and Cumbernauld. Every house in a new town does not need to be a carbon copy of the next; one new town has as many as 150 types of dwellings. There are blocks of flats, single-storey 'flats' for the elderly, and various other kinds of houses, including 'link-building'.

Many people move to a new town from the centre of an old one. They leave a well-developed community and arrive in one which is only just finding its identity. Some are unhappy. They miss old friends and old places, and doctors report a high incidence of 'new town neurosis'. It takes time to put down roots and to build a new life, and probably the success of the new towns lies with the young married couples, starting to bring up their families in this exciting new environment.

10. Planning and Building

58 (*Left*) The construction of Knightsbridge Barracks in London.

59 (*Below*) A 26-storey block of flats in Poplar, East London. Some flats have four rooms as well as a kitchen and bathroom. Notice the service section which contains lifts that connect with the flats by means of covered 'bridges'. But the problems caused by high-rise living mean that most councils are now planning only low- and medium-rise flats.

Architects

The number of houses that can be built on an acre of land (ie 0.404 hectare) varies from a high density of about 18 houses to a low density of 6 or even 4 houses. The surveyor measures and checks the height of the site with theodolites and dumpy levels, and then produces a large-scale map of the area. Architects who design the houses must spend five years studying at a School of Architecture and then two years gaining practical experience before they are fully qualified. Most are members of the Royal Institute of British Architects (RIBA). Their course includes a study of different building methods and materials as well as the problems of installing services such as water, drains, gas, electricity, air-conditioning and central heating.

An architect usually designs a house after the client or builder has given him some idea of the type of house he wants — its size, price, special requirements and so on. Developments are now very varied — some dwellings in a road may be bungalows, while others are detached or semi-detached villas. As well as designing the layout of the house, the architect plans exactly where each house will be sited, and works out how best to fit all the houses into a given area without wasting space, and with each householder having a fair share of the land for gardens.

Think for a few minutes about your own house — where it is built and in which direction it faces. Think about the layout of the rooms — where the doors and windows are, and where the staircase, cupboards and bathroom are placed. Every one of these things had to be carefully thought about by the person who designed your home. The same person also decided with which materials to build the house. Although many houses are designed by architects, some are planned by builders and others still are put up by builders who follow a standard plan which has been used many times before. Most new houses are built on estates. Sometimes each house has the same design, sometimes there are several designs in each road, but for a house of this sort the prospective owner usually has little — if any — say in how the house will look.

The architect draws plans and sketches to show his client what he has in mind. The client may be a speculative builder, who intends to erect hundreds of buildings of the same design, or he may be a prospective owner-occupier. In the latter case the house will be a 'one-off' design and the client will be able to say what sort of house he wants. After the architect and client have reached agreement detailed plans are then drawn and these are sent to the planning committee at the local council. The council's planning officer may require changes to be made if the plan of a building does not fit in well with the rest of the road, or if he feels that something is lacking in the proposed construction. When the plans have been passed the architect supplies working drawings and the builder sets to work on the house. The architect of a one-off building usually visits the site as often as possible to check that all is going well. The

60 An open-plan office at Killingworth New Town in which about 60 architects work in their own separate areas. These areas can be regrouped as work schedules demand.

building inspector at the local council offices approves the plans to ensure that they comply with the building regulations. The working drawings include details of the types of windows, doors, cupboards, wardrobes and other built-in furniture and fireplaces. The architect may give advice on the painting and decoration of the inside and the outside, and may even design the layout of the garden. Paths, drives, lawns, flower-beds, shrubs and perhaps a pool or rockery, carefully planned and sited, greatly enhance the attractiveness of the property. The success of so many garden centres in recent years shows that more people than ever are realizing the importance of a garden.

So far, we have talked solely about architects who design houses. Many architects, however, do not design any houses, but work instead for large architectural firms, which may employ 50 or more people to design large buildings like factories, cinemas, hotels and airports. The architects plan the building as a team. Other technical specialists in the team include a consulting structural engineer who investigates the ground conditions and is responsible for the foundations, a mechanical engineer who designs the heating and air-conditioning, an electrical engineer who designs the lighting, a quantity surveyor who estimates costs, an acoustics consultant with responsibility for noise control, and perhaps a landscape architect.

Building Firms

National contractors each employ thousands of men. Some employ more than 20,000 and work anywhere in the world. Other firms have 300 to 2,000 workers on their books, are sited close to the large cities, and carry out most of their work within a limited area. Many smaller firms also exist throughout Britain. Some employ a handful of men, some as many as 30. They maintain existing buildings, provide extensions and in some cases put up new buildings. Repair work is carried out by small private firms as well as by local authorities.

A large building firm has many departments each specializing in its own field. The two main departments are Production and Servicing:

Production includes

Surveying	—	finding the quantity of materials needed
Estimating	—	analysis of prices
Buying	—	perhaps from abroad
Plant	—	the mechanical engineer supervises transport, concrete mixers, excavators, cranes and hoists.

Servicing includes

Planning	—	the design office employs architects and structural engineers
Programming	—	schemes of work and timetabling
Publicity	—	extensive advertising
Research	—	new types of construction, soil examination, tests on materials, especially concrete.

Tenders

After an architect has designed a building, a number of different builders (perhaps as many as six) are invited to submit a tender to do the work. A tender is an offer to carry out the work for a stated amount of money. The architect sends each of the builders a bill of quantities, including specifications for all the work to be done, and drawings. The bill of quantities is studied carefully, since it tells the builder how much material is needed for the job. It is extremely important to know at this stage exactly how many hundreds of thousands of bricks must be ordered, how much concrete and timber will be used, and what other materials will be required. A quantity surveyor has already worked out these details for the architect, so that the builder — if his tender is accepted — can arrange for the material to be delivered in the right quantity and at the right time. The builder works out how much it will cost him to buy all the quantities specified — perhaps as many as 1,500 different items, from a thousand tonnes of concrete to a bell for the front door — and how much he will have to pay his men to do the work. A total price is reached, onto which is added an amount for profit, and the tender is then sent to the architect. The builder offering the lowest tender usually gets the job.

Demolition

Other buildings, especially in towns, may have to be demolished before new structures can be put up. Sites are restricted in the centre of towns, and the public must be protected by erecting wide timber and wire-mesh screens to catch falling debris and masonry. A heavy steel ball dropped through the roof or swung against the wall by a crane soon demolishes a house. Special vehicles attached to a steel cable are used to pull a wall apart. Explosives are sometimes used to demolish tall chimneys, bridges and large old buildings. Today demolition is easy, but the use of pre-stressed concrete in much modern building will cause dangers and problems for demolition experts in the future. Pre-stressed concrete has steel cables or rods, which have already been stretched (pre-tensioned), inserted in the concrete to strengthen it. The idea was introduced in 1904 by the Frenchman Eugène Freysinnet, and allowed the erection of lighter and stronger buildings than are possible when ordinary metal reinforcing rods are used to strengthen concrete. Such buildings are likely to be still standing hundreds of years from now, because of the great difficulty in knocking them down.

On the Site
Before building can commence, the site is made level and the top soil (later needed for the gardens) is removed by a huge scraper. A builder cannot begin to build houses in the middle of a muddy field without first laying a road along which lorries and heavy equipment can travel easily, and storm drains at the side of the road have, of course, to be constructed before the road itself is laid. The main sewer is sited so that other sewers slope down to it, and manholes lead down to sewer junctions.

The site foreman and his assistant mark out with strong string the exact position of each house to be built. This is an important task, and at least one house has been built back to front because the foreman got things wrong at this stage!

Building Materials
Brick has a coarser grain than stone. Medieval bricks were cast in moulds of the required shape, and the brick chimney-stacks of Hampton Court, for example, were made by this method. Modern bricks are made of clay that has been mixed with water to soften it. The clay is pushed through a rectangular hole on a machine and comes out as a long strip. This is cut to the size of bricks by using wires. The shapes are then heated in a brickyard kiln at about 1,000° Centigrade. There are several different types of bricks. Some (known as commons) come in various shades and are used on inside walls where they will be covered with plaster. More attractive bricks (facings) are used on outside walls. Often they are given a coating of sandy clay before they are put in the kilns and this gives them a regular attractive colour. Foundation bricks, which bear the weight of the building, are made of special clay and fired at 1,400° Centigrade to make them strong and water resistant. Many bricks have holes or hollows (called a frog) on the top and bottom so that the mortar will grip the bricks extra firmly.

Granite, consisting of a compacted mass of hard granules, is the hardest building material used in England. It is worked with hammers, then with pointed chisels and later polished. The ICI building at Millbank has a Cornish granite base.

Concrete is a mixture of sand, cement and small stones called aggregate. Cement was invented by Joseph Aspdin of Gravesend in 1824, and is used to bind the concrete. It is made by crushing limestone or chalk into a powder and then mixing it with clay and water. The amount of gypsum added determines the speed at which the cement will set.

The strength of concrete depends on the proportions of aggregate, sand and cement used, as well as on the size of stones in the aggregate. A mistake in the proportions could result in serious structural defects. On large building sites, there is usually one man whose sole job is to check that the concrete is of the correct strength. A machine called an 'over-silo mixer' weighs the amounts and mixes them thoroughly. A further check is made by the site engineer, who regularly produces concrete cubes during the building process. These cubes are sent to a laboratory where they are tested and compressed to make certain that they are capable of withstanding the various pressures they are intended to bear.

The cement in concrete takes longer to set in cold weather. Ready-mixed cement is now increasingly being used on large sites and is supplied by specialist firms who deliver it in large mixers. This saves time, expense and the space that would be needed for storing dry materials.

Foundations

The foundations and basement for a large building may go as much as 7 metres below ground level. A fleet of lorries is needed to carry away the excavated mud, clay and soil. For instance, a basement 30 by 20 metres, and 7 metres deep, will entail the removal of about 900 lorry-loads of earth.

A thick slab of reinforced concrete may be laid as the foundation, or there may be wide cylindrical holes bored 10 metres or more below the surface and filled with concrete. The number of bore holes, and their depth and width, depend on the soil conditions; usually small holes are bored first to examine the soil.

The Leaning Tower of Pisa in Italy has been slowly toppling over for centuries because it is too heavy for the ground on which it stands. The city of Venice is built on more than 100 man-made islands, with hundreds of thousands of wooden piles driven into the mud and soil to support the foundations of buildings. But the great weight of the city means that Venice is slowly sinking. High-rise buildings are suitable in New York because they are built on rock. But in many other places there are problems. In London, for instance, the clay sub-soil makes it difficult to erect heavy buildings without extensive foundations. One multi-storey office block built at Marble Arch is about 80 metres high, and needed a foundation of 130 reinforced concrete piles. Each of these went 20 metres into the London clay, was 2 metres wide and belled out at the base to 5 metres.

Tower cranes are generally used near the building and a climbing crane is winched up inside the framework of a tall building. This allows the arm to operate freely above the level of construction already reached.

Steel Framing

The steel skeleton of a steel-framed building is bolted into position and the joints are then made secure by steel rivets fixed by pneumatic hammers or welding. The walls are added later. The steel frame is the support for the building, and the walls are only needed for privacy and warmth. They do not have to be particularly strong, and panels of stainless steel, aluminium, plastic or glass can be made in factories and fixed in position when they are needed.

Steel cage structures are often said to be 'clothed' with outer walls. The architect comes along like a dressmaker, and designs 'clothes' to cover the bare steel framework.

Putting up a Building

Here, briefly, are the main tasks involved in putting up a house. First, trenches are dug below the surface and either a concrete base covering the area of the building is laid or the lower parts of the trenches are filled with concrete to ensure a strong base for the brick walls.

The lowest layers, or courses, of engineering bricks are often made of hard, burned brick that is not very porous and does not allow moisture from the ground to rise up the walls. The damp course is built a few courses above the ground. This is a layer of material such as roofing felt which is fixed between two courses. Ventilated bricks allow air to flow under the floor boards.

The outer wall and the inner wall are about 5 centimetres apart and metal ties hold the two walls together. The space between — the cavity — prevents moisture from reaching the inner wall. Often nowadays, to save time and expense, the inner layer is made with breeze blocks.

Sleeper walls support floor joists which in turn support the floor boards. The roof is usually made of timbers cut on the spot, to the required lengths, after which it is covered with roofing felt. Battens (strips of wood) are fastened to the timbers through the felt, and the roofing tiles (slate, clay or concrete) are nailed or placed on these.

Plumbers and electricians fix cables and pipes. Plaster-boards, a 'sandwich' of plaster between two sheets of cardboard, are fixed to form a ceiling and are later covered with a thin layer of plaster. The brick or breeze block walls are also plastered over and the partition walls between rooms are covered with plaster-board.

The window frames and door frames are fixed in position, the doors are hung and the glaziers fix glass in the windows. In the past, local materials were generally used, but cheap transport, branded goods and standard fitments have

61 The Post Office Tower in London is the highest building in Britain. Trunk calls are transmitted by radio to other towers around the country, so overcoming jams on trunk-call cables.

caused local variants to die out. Everywhere standardization abounds.

The painter is then called in, and with the help of a spray gun quickly covers the large surfaces. Meanwhile the plumber installs the bath, washbasin and lavatory, and fixes the sink-unit in the kitchen. Tiles are stuck on the walls in the bathroom and kitchen, while the electrician finishes the cabling of the circuit.

The house is now more or less finished. The whole operation, from laying the first brick to putting on the last brush of paint, given luck and barring hold-ups, may be completed in just a few months.

11. Tomorrow

Recent architecture has pointed the way towards new possibilities in the design of large buildings: the Roman Catholic Cathedral at Liverpool, Guildford Cathedral, the Post Office Tower and Centre Point in London, the Bull-Ring in Birmingham and Piccadilly in Manchester. The idea of pedestrian precincts, which free shopping areas from motor traffic, is also affecting modern architecture.

62 A modern house of glass, concrete and aluminium. The living-room has a split level, with the kitchen at the lower level. The bedrooms and bathroom are downstairs.

Enterprising architects will go on designing pleasing buildings, and new ideas, such as the glass house, will continue to appear. The ordinary home will probably change little in external appearance over the next few decades, but kitchens will probably become larger to make space for double-sinks, dish-washers, and deep-freezers. Utility rooms are now being included as standard in many new homes, and increasing insulation is improving comfort. The Parker Morris standard for housing design has been in operation since the early 1960s, determining minimum house sizes for family groups. The standard is now followed by local authority housing and might well in time improve the standards of private housing developments.

Cities will continue to grow and more new towns will appear, for these centres provide both work and companionship. But much remains to be done before everyone will have a decent house. Many people still live in appalling conditions. In one area of a northern industrial town, tenants complained in 1974:

We have no bathrooms and have to make do with outside toilets. A lot of the houses have not been rewired since they were built in 1927 and they are nothing more than slums. It is a great area with some tremendous community spirit but a lot of people are becoming disillusioned because they think the council is never going to do anything to help.

Britain has a fine heritage in its buildings. Any town or village more than a few hundred years old still contains buildings from practically every generation up to the present time, and it is a matter of national concern that historic structures should be preserved whenever possible.

A group of private individuals founded the National Trust in 1895. It preserves, looks after and opens to the public beautiful places and buildings of special merit. It has more than 1,000 properties in England, Wales and Northern Ireland (Scotland has its own National Trust). The Trust survives on entrance fees paid by the public when they visit the historic houses, and on gifts of money. Property is often donated to the Trust, and it also buys property out of its funds.

The National Trust controls more than 250,000 acres of land, including stretches of coastline, lakes, waterfalls, mountains, forests, moorland and agricultural land. In addition, it owns many buildings — both small and grand — all with a story to tell. One of the Trust's oldest buildings is Old Soar in Kent, part of a thirteenth-century knight's house. Perhaps one of the most well-known buildings in its care is Gibeon's Farm at East Bergholt in Suffolk, which appears in two of Constable's landscapes — 'The Haywain' and 'The Valley Farm'. The Trust even owns several complete villages, such as Chiddingstone in Kent and Selworthy in Somerset.

63 (*Above*) A model of a glass house in which warm air is never lost but instead passes through a machine at the top of the house and feeds the heat into the incoming air.

64 (*Above right*) Most new houses now have large picture windows to let in as much light as possible. Some picture windows, such as the one shown here, cover an entire wall — to make the most of an attractive view and to bring the garden into the house.

65 (*Right*) Part of the beautiful village of Selworthy in Somerset, administered by the National Trust.

The Department of the Environment also looks after many old buildings, abbeys, historic houses and castles, maintains them and opens them to the public.

Many beautiful buildings remain from centuries long gone, but fine buildings are also being designed today. The attitude that everything from the past is good and that buildings of the present are styleless and inelegant is as short-sighted as it is foolish. This book has shown that each age in history had developed its own styles to cater for the needs and tastes of those who had to live and work in these buildings. There is every sign that the twentieth century will be remembered as the age when, for the first time, everyone had come to expect a comfortable, sanitary, convenient and pleasant house in which to live. By the end of the twentieth century, the planners may well have achieved this objective for just about every family in Britain.

Glossary

aisle	the side part of a building, as in a church where it is often separated off by pillars
alcove	a recess in the corner of a room
Art Nouveau	(French term meaning 'New Art') a decorative style popular from about 1890 to 1910
bow window	a curved projecting window
bungalow	a single-storey house
buttress	a strengthening support against an outside wall
casement	a window-pane in a frame which hinges open
cesspool	a hole in the ground for sewage
clerestory	an upper wall with windows
colonnade	a row of columns
conduit	a pipe or channel to carry water, or metal tubing for electrical wires
cornice	a moulding along the top of a wall, where the wall and ceiling join
crenellations	battlements
crescent	a curved street
cruciform	in the shape of a cross
cruck	a primitive form of building where curved beams support the roof and walls
curtain wall	a wall surrounding a castle
dais	a raised platform at one end of a hall
Decorated	a style of Gothic architecture found in England 1250-1350; elaborate and richly decorated, with ornamental open-work
dormer	a window built out from a sloping roof
Early English	a style of architecture, 1150-1250, characterized by tall narrow windows and pointed arches
eaves	the overhanging edge of a roof
elevation	a flat drawing of one side of a building, usually the front
fanlight	a fan-shaped window above a front door
flue	a small narrow chimney
gable	the triangular part of an outside wall which supports the roof

Gothic	a style of architecture with high pointed arches, clustered columns, etc.
gutter	a channel or groove to carry water from the roof
hipped roof	a roof where all the sides slope and there are no gables
inglenook	a space, often recessed, at the side of a fire which has been fitted with seats
jetty	a projecting upper storey of a house
keystone	the central stone of an arch
lancet	a tall narrow window with a pointed arch
lintel	a horizontal beam or stone set over a door or window opening
mosaic	a pattern of small colourful stones set in fine cement
mullion	the upright division in a window
Norman	an early style of architecture, found in England 1070-1150, characterized by small rounded windows and deeply recessed doorways
pargetting	plaster spread over the outside of a house and moulded into decorative patterns
parquet	a floor made of small blocks of wood placed to form a pattern
pediment	a decorative triangle placed over a portico
Perpendicular	a style of architecture found in England 1350-1550, characterized by tall uncluttered windows, four-centred arches and panelled walls
portico	a porch formed by pillars
pointing	the finished joint between bricks or masonry
rafter	a sloping beam supporting the roof
sash	a window-frame that slides up and down
semi-detached	a house joined by a party wall to one other house only
shingles	wooden tiles
stucco	plaster used on an outside wall
terrace	a row of houses joined together
terracotta	burned clay
transept	a section of a church at right angles to the main east-west line
vault	an arched roof or ceiling; also a cellar
vestibule	an ante-room
wainscot	wood panelling on an inside wall
weather-boarding	overlapping boards on an outside wall

Further Reading

A Allen, *The Story of Your Home* (Faber)

A Barfoot, *Homes in Britain* (Batsford)

L and W Ison, *English Architecture Through the Ages* (Barker)

J Harvey, *Man the Builder* (Priory Press)

K Lindley, *Chapels and Meeting Houses* (John Baker)

P Maguire, *From Tree Dwellings to New Towns* (Longman)

H E Priestley, *The English Home* (Muller)

F Schaffer, *The New Town Story* (Paladin)

R R Sellman, *Castles and Fortresses* (Methuen)

D Yarwood, *English Houses* (Batsford)

Index

Numbers in **bold** refer to the figure numbers of the illustrations.